PRIMARY MATHEMATICS 6B

Third Edition

Primary Mathematics Project Team

Project Director
Dr Kho Tek Hong

Team Members
Chee Kum Hoong, Hector
Liang Hin Hoon
Lim Eng Tann
Lim Hui Cheng, Rosalind
Ng Hwee Wan
Ng Siew Lee
Thong Chee Hing

Curriculum Specialist
Cheong Ngan Peng, Christina

Curriculum Planning & Development Division
Ministry of Education, Singapore

FEDERAL PUBLICATIONS
An imprint of Times Media

Published by
Times Media Private Limited
A member of the Times Publishing Group
Times Centre, 1 New Industrial Road, Singapore 536196
E-mail: fps@tpl.com.sg
Online Book Store: http://www.timesone.com.sg/fpl

First published   1985
Second Edition 1996
Third Edition   2000
Reprinted   2000, 2001, 2003

ISBN 981-01-8084-5

Printed by Times Offset (M) Sdn. Bhd

Illustrator
Yin Lu

ACKNOWLEDGEMENTS

The project team would like to record their thanks to the following:

- members of the Primary Mathematics Team who developed the first edition and second edition of the package

- members of the Steering Committee for the second edition of the package

- teachers who tested the materials in the package and provided useful insights and suggestions

- Educational Technology Division, for the design and production of the audio-visual components of the package

- all those who have helped in one way or another in the development and production of the package

PREFACE

The Primary Mathematics package comprises textbooks, workbooks, teacher's guides and audio-visual materials.

The main feature of the package is the use **Concrete** ➡ **Pictorial** ➡ **Abstract** approach. The pupils are provided with the necessary learning experiences beginning with the concrete and pictorial stages, followed by the abstract stage to enable them to learn mathematics meaningfully. Like the previous editions of the package, this edition encourages active thinking processes, communication of mathematical ideas and problem solving.

This textbook is accompanied by a workbook and a teacher's guide. It comprises 5 units. Each unit is divided into parts: ❶, ❷, . . . Each part starts with a meaningful situation for communication and is followed by specific learning tasks numbered 1, 2, . . . The sign | Workbook Exercise ⟩ is used to link the textbook to the workbook exercises.

Practice exercises are designed to provide the pupils with further practice after they have done the relevant workbook exercises. Review exercises and revision exercises are provided for cumulative reviews of concepts and skills. All the practice exercises, review exercises and revision exercises are optional exercises. Answers to the practice exercises and review exercises are given at the back of the textbook.

The colour patch ■ is used to invite active participation from the pupils and to facilitate oral discussion. The pupils are advised not to write on the colour patches.

Challenging word problems are marked with *. Teachers may encourage the abler pupils to attempt them.

CONTENTS

1 **Circles**
1   Radius and Diameter   6
2   Circumference   10
     PRACTICE 1A   14
3   Area   15
     PRACTICE 1B   20
     PRACTICE 1C   21

2 **Graphs**
1   Pie Charts   22

REVIEW A   **26**

REVIEW B   **32**

3 **Volume**
1   Solving Problems   38
     PRACTICE 3A   43
     PRACTICE 3B   44
     PRACTICE 3C   45

4 **Triangles and 4-sided Figures**
1   Finding Unknown Angles   46
     PRACTICE 4A   50
     PRACTICE 4B   51

REVIEW C   **52**

REVIEW D   **57**

REVIEW E   **62**

5   * More Challenging Word Problems

1	Whole Numbers and Decimals	67
	PRACTICE 5A	71
2	Fractions	72
	PRACTICE 5B	76
	PRACTICE 5C	77
3	Ratio	78
	PRACTICE 5D	81
	PRACTICE 5E	82
4	Percentage	83
	PRACTICE 5F	85
5	Speed	86
	PRACTICE 5G	89

REVIEW F   **90**

REVIEW G   **95**

ANSWERS   **101**

1 Circles

1 Radius and Diameter

Draw a circle using a pair of compasses.

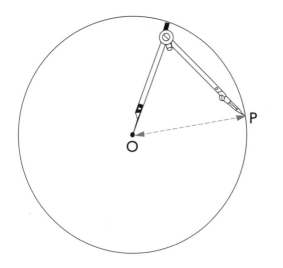

O is the **centre** of the circle.
OP is a **radius** of the circle.

Then draw a straight line MP which passes through the centre of the circle.

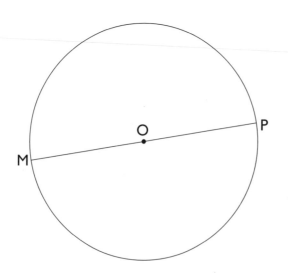

MP is a **diameter** of the circle.

Is MP twice as long as OP?

1. Measure the radius of each circle.

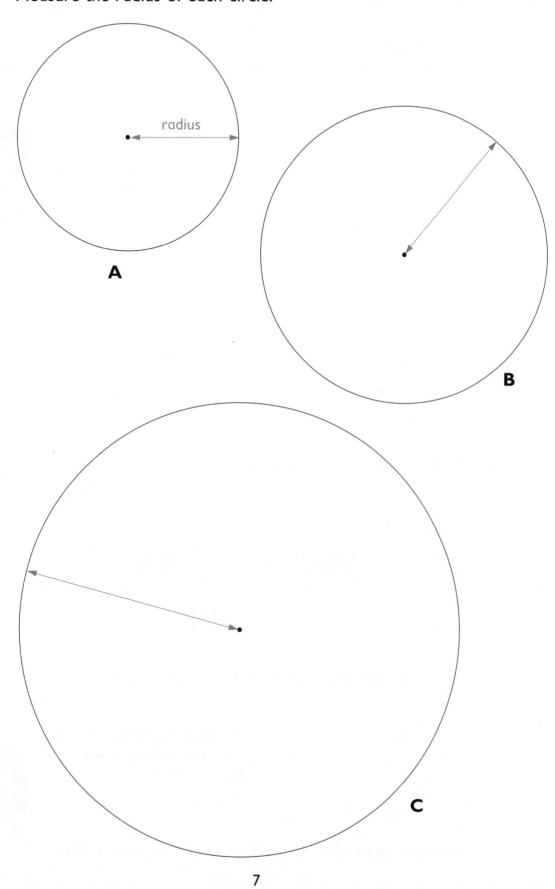

radius

A

B

C

2. Measure the radius and diameter of the circle.

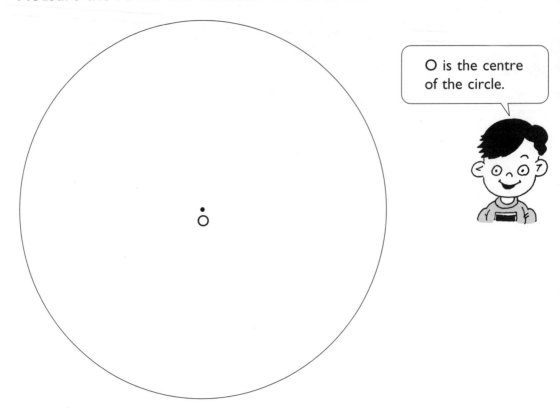

O is the centre of the circle.

3. (a) Fold a paper circle like this:

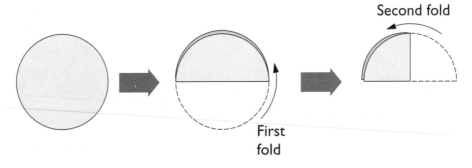

Second fold

First fold

Then unfold the paper circle to find its centre.

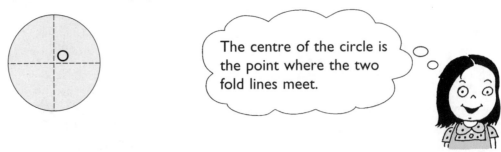

The centre of the circle is the point where the two fold lines meet.

(b) Measure the radius and diameter of the paper circle.

> Diameter = 2 × Radius
> Radius = Diameter ÷ 2

4. Draw a circle of radius 5 cm.

5. Draw a circle of diameter 8 cm.

6. (a) The radius of the circle is 4 cm.
   Find its diameter.

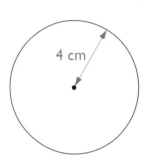

(b) The diameter of the circle is 18 cm.
   Find its radius.

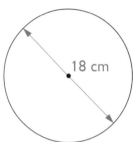

7. The following circles are not drawn to scale.

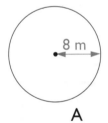 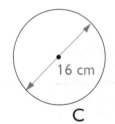 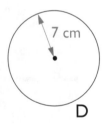

| A | B | C | D |

(a) Which circle is the biggest?
(b) Which circle is the smallest?
(c) Copy and complete the table:

Circle	Radius	Diameter
A	8 m	
B		20 m
C		16 cm
D	7 cm	

Workbook Exercise 1

2 Circumference

Use a string to measure the **circumference** of a circle like this:

> The **circumference** of a circle is its perimeter.

> The circumference of a circle is slightly more than 3 times its diameter.

1. Aziz measured the diameter and the circumference of three circles. He recorded the results as follows:

Circle	Diameter	Circumference
A	5 cm	15.7 cm
B	7 cm	22 cm
C	10 cm	31.4 cm

Find the value of **circumference ÷ diameter** for each circle. What do you notice?

The circumference of each circle is about 3.14 times the diameter.

The value of **circumference ÷ diameter** is the same for any circle. This value is represented by π.

$\pi \approx 3.14$ or $\frac{22}{7}$

Circumference of circle = $\pi \times$ Diameter

2. The diameter of a hoop is 60 cm. Find its circumference.
   (Take $\pi = 3.14$)

Circumference = $\pi \times 60$

   = 3.14×60

   = ■ cm

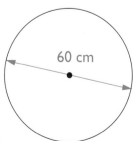

60 cm

3. The radius of a disc is 25 cm. Find its circumference. (Take π = 3.14)

Diameter = 2 × 25

= 50 cm

Circumference = π × 50

= 3.14 × 50

= ■ cm

25 cm

4. The radius of a wheel is 14 cm. Find its circumference.

$\left(\text{Take } \pi = \dfrac{22}{7} \right)$

Diameter = 28 cm

Circumference = π × 28

= $\dfrac{22}{7}$ × 28

= ■ cm

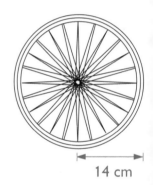

14 cm

5. Find the circumference of a circle of diameter 70 cm. $\left(\text{Take } \pi = \dfrac{22}{7} \right)$

6. Find the circumference of a circle of radius 4 m. (Take π = 3.14)

7. Find the circumference of each circle. $\left(\text{Take } \pi = \dfrac{22}{7} \right)$

(a)

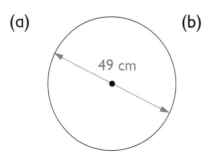

49 cm

(b)

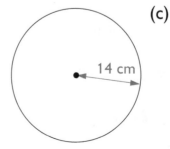

14 cm

(c)

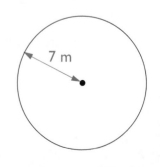

7 m

8. Find the circumference of each circle. (Take π = 3.14)

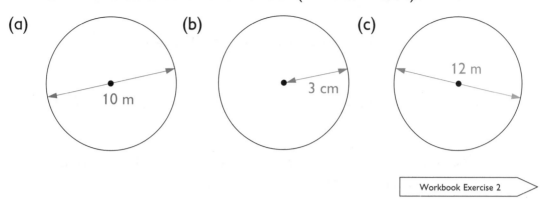

(a)

10 m

(b)

3 cm

(c)

12 m

Workbook Exercise 2

9. The figure shows a flowerbed which has the shape of a **semicircle**. Find its perimeter. (Take π = 3.14)

4 m

A **semicircle** is a half circle.

10. A wire is bent to form three semicircles as shown. Find the length of the wire in terms of π.

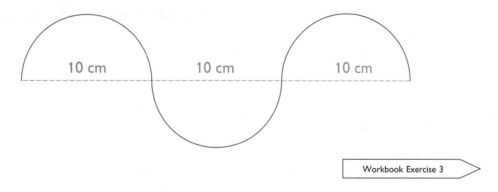

10 cm   10 cm   10 cm

Workbook Exercise 3

11. The figure is made up of a rectangle and two semicircles. Find its perimeter. $\left(\text{Take } \pi = \dfrac{22}{7}\right)$

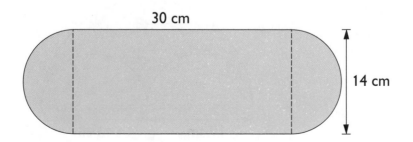

30 cm

14 cm

PRACTICE 1A

1. Find the circumference of a circle of diameter 20 cm. (Take π = 3.14)

2. Find the circumference of a circle of radius 35 cm. $\left(\text{Take } \pi = \dfrac{22}{7}\right)$

3. The diameter of a circular plate is 23 cm. What is its circumference? Give your answer correct to 1 decimal place. (Take π = 3.14)

4. The figure shows a circle within a square. Find the circumference of the circle. (Take π = 3.14)

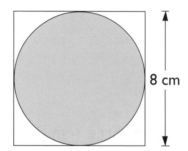

8 cm

5. What is the length of this curve which is made up of four equal semicircles? $\left(\text{Take } \pi = \dfrac{22}{7}\right)$

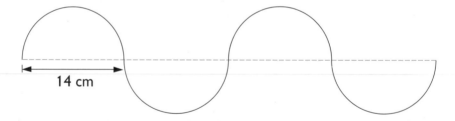

14 cm

6. The figure is made up of 3 semicircles. Find its perimeter in terms of π.

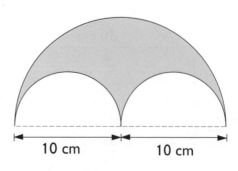

10 cm   10 cm

③ Area

The radius of the circle is 10 cm. Estimate its area.

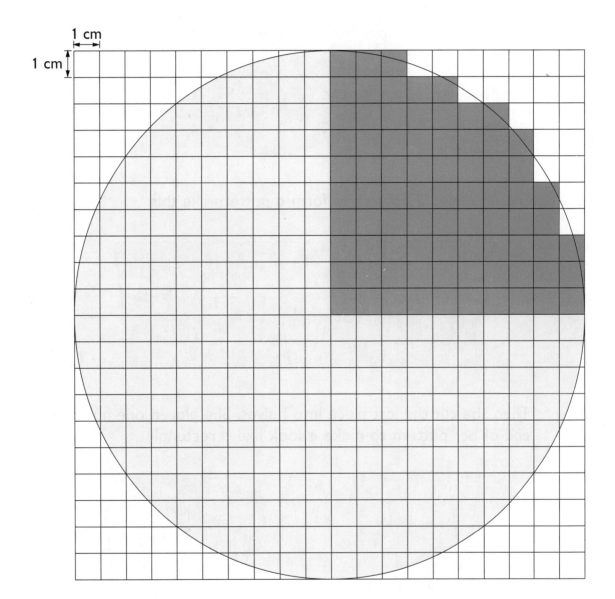

Area of $\frac{1}{4}$ of the circle $\approx$ 79 cm²

Area of the circle $\approx$ 4 × 79

$$= 316 \text{ cm}^2$$

1. Eva cut a circle into 24 equal pieces.

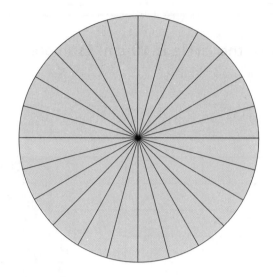

She arranged 23 pieces to form a pattern like this:

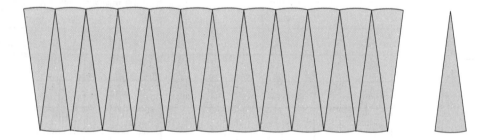

Then she cut the last piece into halves. She placed one half at each end of her pattern to make it look like a rectangle.

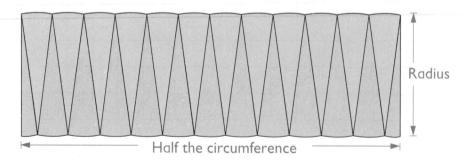

Radius

Half the circumference

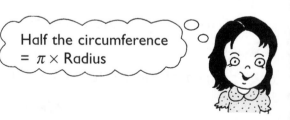

Half the circumference
= $\pi \times$ Radius

> Area of circle = π × Radius × Radius

Taking π = 3.14, find the area of a circle of radius 10 cm.

Area of circle = π × 10 × 10
$\quad\quad\quad\quad$ = 3.14 × 10 × 10
$\quad\quad\quad\quad$ = ■ cm²

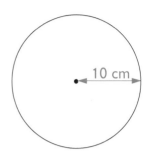

2. The radius of a circle is 14 cm. Find its area. $\left(\text{Take } \pi = \dfrac{22}{7} \right)$

Area of circle = π × 14 × 14

$\quad\quad\quad\quad$ = $\dfrac{22}{7}$ × 14 × 14

$\quad\quad\quad\quad$ = ■ cm²

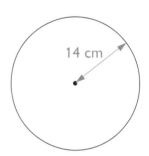

3. The diameter of a circle is 8 cm. Find its area. (Take π = 3.14)

Radius = 8 ÷ 2 = 4 cm
Area = π × 4 × 4
$\quad\quad$ = ■ cm²

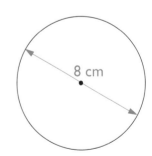

4. Find the area of a circle of radius 7 m. $\left(\text{Take } \pi = \dfrac{22}{7} \right)$

5. Find the area of a circle of diameter 12 m. (Take π = 3.14)

17

6. Find the area of each circle. $\left(\text{Take } \pi = \dfrac{22}{7} \right)$

(a)

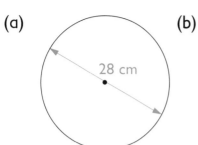

28 cm

(b)

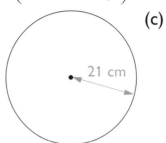

21 cm

(c)

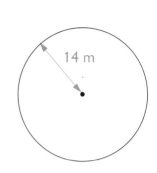

14 m

7. Find the area of each circle. (Take π = 3.14)

(a)

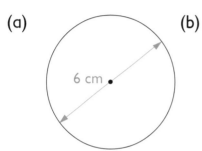

6 cm

(b)

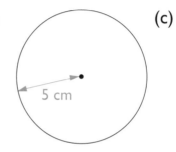

5 cm

(c)

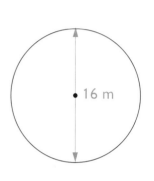

16 m

Workbook Exercise 4

8. Find the area of each semicircular shape. (Take π = 3.14)

(a)

12 cm

(b)

20 cm

9. Each of the following figures is in a shape of a quarter circle. Find its area. (Take π = 3.14)

(a)

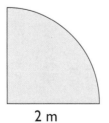

2 m

(b)

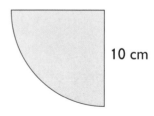

10 cm

Workbook Exercise 5

10. The shaded parts in the following figures are quarter circles. Find the total shaded area in each figure. (Take $\pi = 3.14$)

(a)

(b)

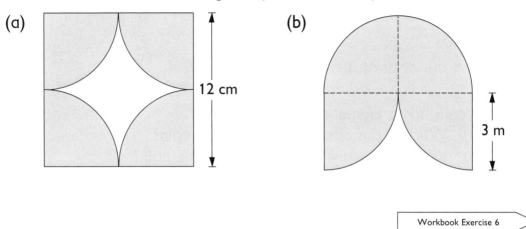

Workbook Exercise 6

11. The figure is made up of a semicircle, a rectangle and a triangle. Find its area. (Take $\pi = 3.14$)

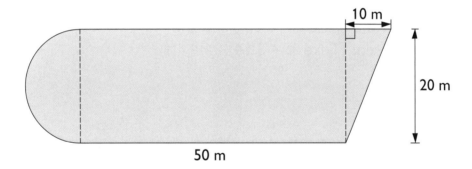

12. The figure shows two semicircles. Find the area of the shaded part in terms of π.

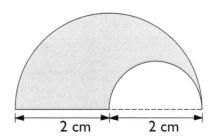

Workbook Exercises 7 & 8

PRACTICE 1B

1. Find the area of a circle of radius 6 cm. (Take π = 3.14)

2. Find the area of a circle of diameter 28 m. $\left(\text{Take } \pi = \dfrac{22}{7} \right)$

3. A coin has a diameter of 4 cm.
   (a) What is the circumference of the coin?
   (b) What is the area of one face of the coin?
   (Take π = 3.14)

4. Mr Li has a semicircular flowerbed. The straight side is 2 m long. What is the area of the flowerbed? (Take π = 3.14)

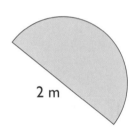

2 m

5. $\dfrac{1}{4}$ of the circle is shaded. If the radius of the circle is 10 cm, find the shaded area. (Take π = 3.14)

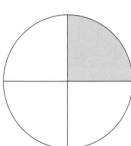

6. The figure shows a circle within a square. If the area of the square is 36 cm², find the area and circumference of the circle. (Take π = 3.14)

7. The figure is made up of 4 quarter circles. Find its area. $\left(\text{Take } \pi = \dfrac{22}{7} \right)$

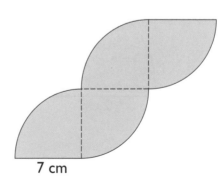

7 cm

PRACTICE 1C

1. A table mat is made up of a square and 4 semicircles as shown.
   (a) What is the area of the table mat?
   (b) What is its perimeter?

   $$\left(\text{Take } \pi = \frac{22}{7} \right)$$

   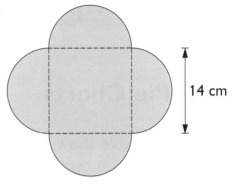

   14 cm

2. The figure is made up of a triangle and a semicircle. Find its area and perimeter. (Take $\pi = 3.14$)

   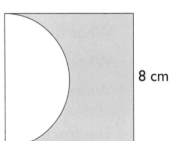

   6 m

   8 m

   10 m

3. The figure shows a square and a semicircle. Find the area and perimeter of the shaded part. (Take $\pi = 3.14$)

   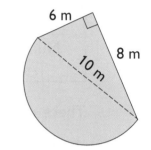

   8 cm

4. The figure is made up of two semicircles and a quarter circle. Find its area and perimeter. Leave your answers in terms of π.

   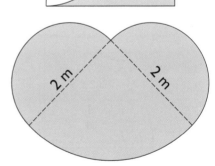

   2 m   2 m

5. The figure shows 2 circles. Find the area of the shaded part in terms of π.

   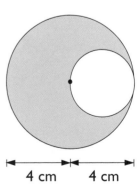

   4 cm   4 cm

2 Graphs

1 Pie Charts

The table shows the number of T-shirts of different sizes sold in a shop on a certain day.

Size	S	M	L	XL
Number of T-shirts	9	18	6	3

There are 36 T-shirts altogether.

$\frac{1}{4}$ of them are of size S.

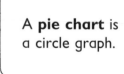

$\frac{9}{36} = \frac{1}{4}$

What fraction of the T-shirts are of size M?

What fraction of the T-shirts are of size L?

What fraction of the T-shirts are of size XL?

The fractions can be shown like this:

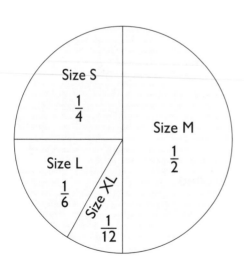

Size S $\frac{1}{4}$

Size M $\frac{1}{2}$

Size L $\frac{1}{6}$

Size XL $\frac{1}{12}$

A **pie chart** is a circle graph.

This is a **pie chart**. It represents the number of T-shirts of different sizes sold in the shop.

1. There are 200 chairs in a warehouse. 80 of them are plastic chairs, 30 are metal chairs, 40 are rattan chairs and the rest are wooden chairs. The pie chart represents the number of chairs of each type.

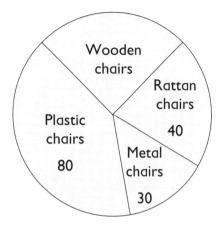

   (a) Which type of chair is found in the greatest quantity?
   (b) How many wooden chairs are there?
   (c) What fraction of the chairs are plastic chairs?
   (d) How many times as many plastic chairs as rattan chairs are there?

2. The pie chart represents the amount of money collected by various stalls at a funfair.

   (a) What fraction of the total amount of money was collected by the games stalls?
   (b) What was the total amount of money collected by the various stalls?
   (c) How much money was collected by the music stalls?
   (d) What was the ratio of the money collected by the food stalls to the money collected by the handicraft stalls?

Workbook Exercise 9

3.   A group of 40 boys were asked to choose bread, rice, porridge or cake for breakfast on a certain day. The pie chart represents their choices.

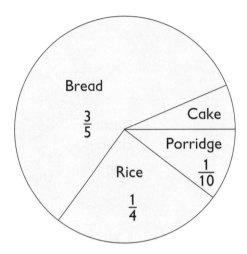

(a)   Which type of breakfast did most pupils have on that day?
(b)   What fraction of the pupils had cake for breakfast?
(c)   How many pupils had bread for breakfast?
(d)   What percentage of the pupils had rice for breakfast?

4.   The pupils in a school were asked to name their favourite subject. The pie chart represents their choices.

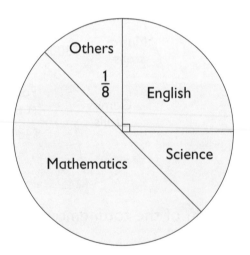

(a)   What fraction of the pupils liked Mathematics?
(b)   What percentage of the pupils liked English?
(c)   What fraction of the pupils liked Science?
(d)   If 1200 pupils liked Mathematics, how many pupils liked English?

Workbook Exercise 10

5. A group of 200 pupils were asked to name their favourite sport. The pie chart represents their choices.

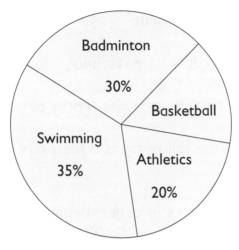

(a) Which was the most popular sport?
(b) What percentage of the pupils chose basketball?
(c) How many pupils chose badminton?
(d) What fraction of the pupils chose swimming?

6. Mrs Chen spent some money on clothes. The pie chart shows how the money was spent.

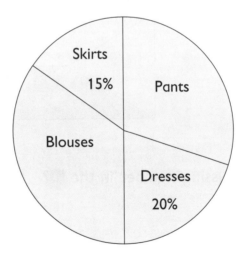

(a) What did Mrs Chen spend the most money on?
(b) What percentage of the money was spent on blouses?
(c) What percentage of the money was spent on pants?
(d) If Mrs Chen spent $60 on pants, how much did she spend altogether?

Workbook Exercise 11

REVIEW A

1. Write 2 340 000 in words.

2. Write 57 hundredths as a decimal.

3. In 435.26, which digit is in the tenths place?

4. Which one of the following is a factor of 119?
    3,   7,   9,   11

5. Arrange the numbers in order, beginning with the smallest.
    0.25,   0.5,   0.09,   0.123

6. Which one of the following is 6 kg when rounded off to the nearest kilogram?
    5.49 kg,   5.399 kg,   5.59 kg,   5.499 kg

7. Express 0.125 as a fraction in its simplest form.

8. What fraction of the rectangle is shaded?

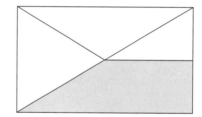

9. What is the missing number in the ■?

    $$\frac{12}{5} = ■ + \frac{2}{5}$$

10. Find the value of 20.6 + 0.89.

11. Find the value of 6.07 × 99.

12. Find the value of 293 ÷ 7 correct to 2 decimal places.

13. Find the value of 15 ÷ 3 + (9 − 6) × 4.

26

14. Which one of the following is the best estimate of the value of 48.59 × 698?

350,   3500,   35 000,   350 000

15. What is the number indicated by the arrow?

16. (a) Express $1\frac{1}{3}$ hours in minutes.

(b) Express 0.02 kg in grams.

17. How many 250-ml packets of apple juice must Mrs Chen buy in order to fill up a jug of capacity 2 litres?

18. Mrs Wu had 30 jars of tarts. She sold all of them at 3 jars for $20. How much money did she receive altogether?

19. A box contained 72 red marbles and blue marbles. There were 20 more red marbles than blue marbles. How many blue marbles were there?

20. An empty basket weighs 0.4 kg. The basket together with 5 mangoes weighs 2 kg. Find the average weight of the mangoes.

21. Sally's weight is 36 kg. Jane is 4 kg heavier than Sally. Find their average weight.

22. The average weight of 3 boys is 35.6 kg. If one of them weighs 34.8 kg, find the average weight of the other two boys.

23. Muthu spent $\frac{2}{5}$ of his money on food and $\frac{1}{4}$ of it on transport. What fraction of his money had he left?

24. In a class, $\frac{1}{3}$ of the pupils are girls. $\frac{1}{2}$ of the boys and $\frac{1}{3}$ of the girls can swim. What fraction of the pupils in the class can swim?

25. Minghua spent $\frac{1}{8}$ of his money on a book and $50 on a radio. He had $\frac{1}{4}$ of his money left. How much money had he left?

26. The ratio of the number of boys to the number of girls at a mass drill is 3 : 4. If there are 270 boys, how many girls are there?

27. There are 36 children in a dance class. The ratio of the number of boys to the number of girls is 5 : 4. How many more boys than girls are there?

28. $\frac{3}{4}$ of Peter's stamps are Singapore stamps. The rest are Malaysian stamps. What percentage of his stamps are Malaysian stamps?

29. The price of a bicycle has increased from $200 to $250. By what percentage has the price increased?

30. The usual price of a badminton racket is $40. It is sold at a discount of 30%. Find the selling price.

31. Mr Chen is driving at a speed of 60 km/h. How far will he travel in 2 hours?

32. The rental rates for a holiday chalet are as follows:

Weekdays	$50 per day
Saturdays & Sundays	$70 per day

Mr Raja and his family stayed at the chalet from Thursday to Sunday. How much did they have to pay?

33. At a sale, Peter bought 4 books and John bought 7 books. John paid $1.95 more than Peter. If all the books were of the same price, how much did they pay altogether?

34. Mary gave $300 of her monthly salary to her parents. She spent $\frac{1}{2}$ of the remainder on food and $120 on transport. If she had $160 left, find her monthly salary.

35. $\frac{3}{4}$ of a sum of money is $1800. How much is $\frac{2}{5}$ of the sum of money?

36. Gopal has 3 times as much money as Raju. If Gopal's money is halved and Raju's money is doubled, what will be the ratio of Gopal's money to Raju's money?

37. Each month, Huili gives 70% of her salary to her parents. She spends 40% of the remainder and saves the rest. If she saves $360, how much is her monthly salary?

38. Ali, John and Peter shared a sum of money. Ali received 40% of the money. The ratio of John's share to Peter's share was 1 : 3. If Peter received $90 more than John, how much money did Ali receive?

39. John took 4 hours to cycle $\frac{3}{5}$ of a journey. He took 2 hours to cycle the remaining 30 km. Find his average speed for the whole journey.

40. If $p = 3$, find the value of

    (a) $\dfrac{10 - p}{p}$

    (b) $5p^2 - 9$

41. The average weight of 3 boxes is x kg. If one of them weighs 2 kg, find the average weight of the other two boxes in terms of x.

42. A square has the same perimeter as the triangle.
Find the area of the square.

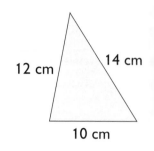

12 cm   14 cm

10 cm

43. The figure is made up of a square and a semicircle.
Find its perimeter. (Take $\pi = 3.14$)

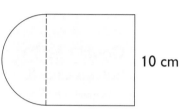

10 cm

44. Each of the following figures is made up of 6 squares. Which figure
does not have a line of symmetry?

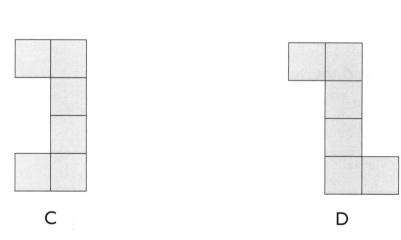

A

B

C

D

45. Copy the shape on dotted paper. Then use the shape to make a tessellation.

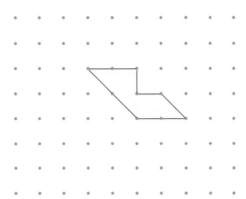

46. The bar graph shows the daily attendance of a class of 40 pupils.

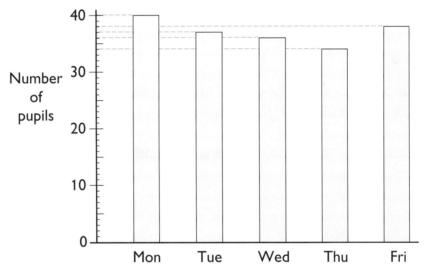

(a) On which day was the attendance the lowest?

(b) What percentage of the pupils were absent on Friday?

(c) What was the average daily attendance?

47. A group of pupils were asked to name their favourite activity in school. The pie chart represents their choices.

(a) What percentage of the pupils liked the school band?

(b) What fraction of the pupils liked swimmimg?

(c) If 18 pupils liked the art club, find the total number of pupils in the group.

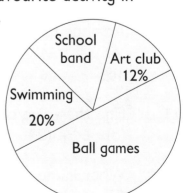

REVIEW B

1. In 6 543 000, what is the digit in the ten thousands place?

2. What is the missing number in the ■?
   630 508 = 630 × ■ + 508

3. What is the missing number in each ■?
   (a) The digit 3 in 837 405 stands for 3 × ■.
   (b) The value of the digit 6 in 2.067 is ■.

4. Which one of the following has 4 as a factor?
   27,   36,   58,   62

5. Write $2 + \dfrac{8}{15}$ as a decimal correct to 2 decimal places.

6. Which one of the following numbers is nearest to 9?
   9.03,   9.09,   9.009,   9.1

7. What fraction of the rectangle is shaded?

8. What is the missing number in the ■?

   $3.004 = 3 + \dfrac{4}{■}$

9. Express each of the following as a fraction in its simplest form.
   (a) 0.048   (b) 36%

10. Arrange the fractions in order, beginning with the smallest.
    $\dfrac{62}{100}$, $\dfrac{31}{20}$, $\dfrac{3}{5}$, $\dfrac{12}{25}$

11. Find the value of each of the following:
    (a) 64 − (24 − 18) × 10   (b) 8 + 16 ÷ 2 × 4

12. What is the missing number in the ■?
    6.5 ÷ ■ = 0.065

13. A shop is open from 10.15 a.m. to 9.30 p.m. How long is the shop open?

14. $\frac{3}{4}$ litre of milk can fill 4 glasses. How many glasses can 3 litres of milk fill?

15. Mrs Li had 1 kg 300 g of mushrooms. She used 450 g for cooking soup. How much mushrooms had she left?

16. At a fruit stall, oranges are sold at 5 for $2. How many oranges can Mrs Raja buy with $24?

17. At a department store, a gift voucher is given for every $40 spent. If Mrs Li buys an oven which costs $350, how many gift vouchers will she get?

18. Rahim sent some postcards to Malaysia. The postage for each postcard was 30¢. If he spent a total of $4.80 on postage, how many postcards did he send?

19. The average of three numbers is 45. If the average of two of the numbers is 47, what is the third number?

20. Water flows from a tap into an empty tank at the rate of 8 litres per minute. How long will it take to fill up the tank if its capacity is 200 litres?

21. Susan bought $\frac{1}{2}$ of a pizza. She ate $\frac{2}{3}$ of the pizza she bought. What fraction of a whole pizza had she left?

22. Hassan spent $\frac{1}{4}$ of his money on a book and $\frac{1}{2}$ of the remainder on a photo album. What fraction of his money did he spend altogether?

23. Find the missing number in each ■.
    (a) 3 : 8 = ■ : 32   (b) 2 : 5 : ■ = 14 : 35 : 49

24. A rope 60 m long is cut into three pieces in the ratio 3 : 2 : 7. What is the length of the longest piece?

25. The number of pupils in a school has increased from 2500 to 2800. By what percentage has the number increased?

26. Peter has 600 Singapore stamps and 200 foreign stamps. What percentage of his stamps are Singapore stamps?

27. Find the value of 15% of $30.

28. Raju took 40 seconds to swim 50 m. Find his average speed in m/s.

29. Samy had 130 stickers and Devi had 50 stickers. After Samy gave Devi some stickers, Samy had twice as many stickers as Devi. How many stickers did Samy give Devi?

30. Gopal bought 100 greeting cards for $60. He sold $\frac{3}{5}$ of them at 3 for $2. He sold the rest at 75¢ each. How much money did he make?

31. $\frac{1}{3}$ of the beads in a box are red, $\frac{2}{3}$ of the remainder are blue and the rest are yellow. If there are 24 red beads, how many yellow beads are there?

32. In a school band, $\frac{1}{2}$ of the members were boys. At the end of the year, 8 girls left the band and the ratio of the number of boys to the number of girls was 4 : 3. How many girls remained in the band?

33. The ratio of John's weight to Peter's weight is 5 : 3. Their average weight is 40 kg. Find John's weight.

34. Mary's savings is $\frac{3}{5}$ of Susan's savings. If Susan saves $60 more than Mary, how much money do they save altogether?

35. In a class, 60% of the pupils are boys. 10% of the boys and 30% of the girls walk to school. What percentage of the pupils in the class walk to school?

36. John saved $75 in January and $60 in February. How many per cent more did he save in January than in February?

37. Mr Li drove for 40 minutes at an average speed of 90 km/h. Then he drove for 20 minutes to complete the remaining 25 km. Find his average speed for the whole journey.

38. The figure is made up of a rectangle and a triangle. The area of the rectangle is 72 cm². Find the area of the triangle.

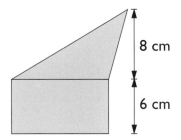

8 cm

6 cm

39. A quarter circle is cut off from a triangle as shown. Find the area of the remaining figure. $\left(\text{Take } \pi = \dfrac{22}{7} \right)$

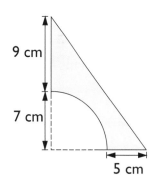

9 cm

7 cm

5 cm

40. The figure shows two quarter circles within a square. Find the perimeter of the shaded part. (Take π = 3.14)

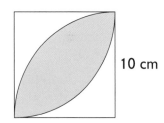

10 cm

41. Copy the symmetric figure on a square grid. Then draw a line of symmetry of the figure.

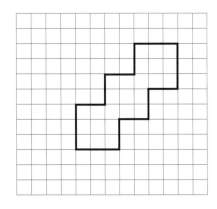

35

42. The figure shows a solid that is made up of unit cubes. At least how many unit cubes are needed to add onto the solid to complete a cuboid?

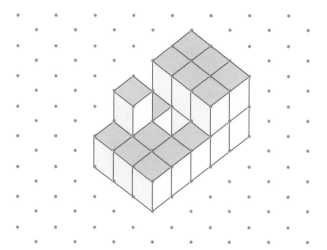

43. This figure shows a solid.

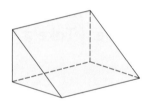

Which one of the following is a net of the solid?

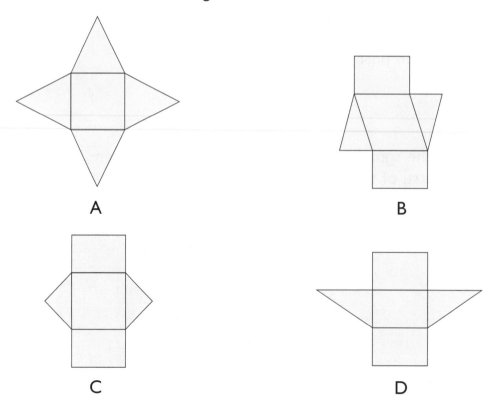

A

B

C

D

44. A group of pupils were asked to choose the uniformed group they would like to join. The pie chart represents their choices.

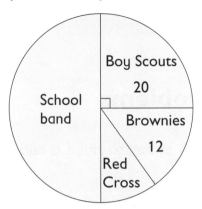

(a) How many pupils chose the school band?
(b) What percentage of the pupils chose Boy Scouts?
(c) How many pupils chose Red Cross?
(d) How many pupils were there in the group?

45. The line graph shows the sales of T-shirts over 5 months.

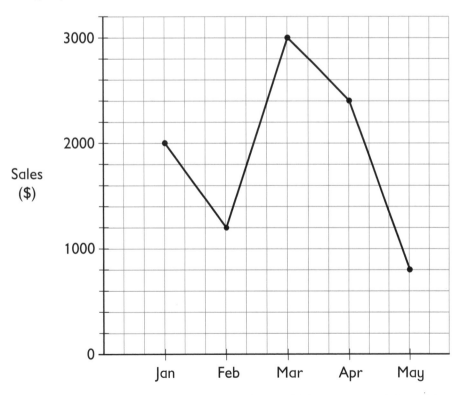

(a) What was the increase in sales from February to March?
(b) What was the average monthly sales?
(c) If each T-shirt was sold for $4 in April, how many T-shirts were sold that month?

3 Volume

1 Solving Problems

Mingde uses 1-cm cubes to build a cube of edge 4 cm. How many cubes does he use?

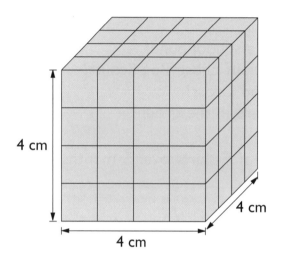

$4 \times 4 \times 4$

How many 1-cm cubes does he need to build a cube of edge 5 cm?

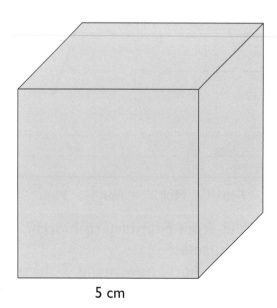

5 cm

If he builds a cube with 729 pieces of 1-cm cubes, find the edge of the cube.

1. The figure shows a solid consisting of 10 cubes of edge 2 cm. Find its volume.

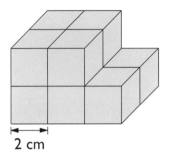

2 cm

2. How many cubes of edge 2 cm are needed to build a cuboid measuring 10 cm by 10 cm by 6 cm?

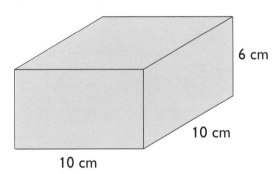

6 cm

10 cm

10 cm

3. The base of a cuboid measures 20 cm by 12 cm. If the volume of the cuboid is 3600 cm³, find its height.

Height = $\dfrac{3600}{20 \times 12}$

= ▪ cm

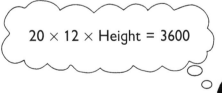

20 × 12 × Height = 3600

Workbook Exercise 12

4. A rectangular container measuring 20 cm by 20 cm by 22 cm is $\frac{1}{2}$ filled with oil. Find the volume of the oil in litres.
(1 litre = 1000 cm³)

Height of oil level = 22 ÷ 2
= 11 cm

Volume of oil = 20 × 20 × 11
= 4400 cm³
= ■ ℓ

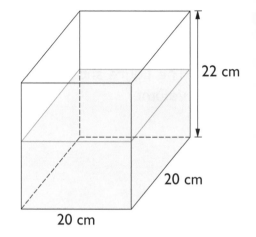

22 cm

20 cm

20 cm

5. A rectangular tank is 90 cm long and 50 cm wide. It contains 162 litres of water when it is $\frac{2}{3}$ full. Find the height of the tank.
(1 litre = 1000 cm³)

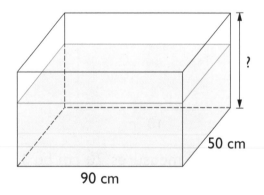

?

50 cm

90 cm

Volume of water = 162 ℓ
= 162 × 1000 cm³

Height of water level = $\dfrac{162 \times 1000}{90 \times 50}$
= ■ cm

Height of the tank = ■ cm

Workbook Exercise 13

6. A rectangular tank, 35 cm long and 25 cm wide, contained some water and a stone. The height of the water level was 10 cm. When the stone was taken out, the water level dropped to 8 cm. Find the volume of the stone.

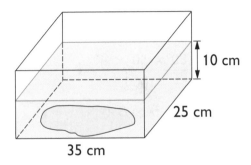

Decrease in height of water level = 10 − 8 = 2 cm

Volume of the stone = 35 × 25 × 2 = ■ cm³

7. A rectangular tank measuring 50 cm by 40 cm by 40 cm is $\frac{1}{2}$ filled with water. When 3 metal cubes of edge 10 cm are placed in the tank, the water level rises. Find the height of the new water level.

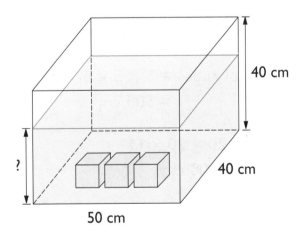

Volume of 3 metal cubes = 10 × 10 × 10 × 3 = 3000 cm³

Increase in height of water level = $\dfrac{3000}{50 \times 40}$ = ■ cm

Height of the new water level = ■ cm

Workbook Exercise 14

8. A rectangular tank measures 80 cm by 50 cm by 60 cm. It is filled with water to its brim. If the water is drained out at a rate of 12 litres per minute, how long will it take to empty the tank? (1 litre = 1000 cm³)

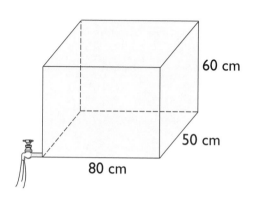

Volume of water = 80 × 50 × 60 cm³

$$= \frac{80 \times 50 \times 60}{1000} \ell$$

$$= 8 \times 5 \times 6 \; \ell$$

Time taken $= \dfrac{8 \times 5 \times 6}{12}$

= ■ min

9. 4 metal cubes of edge 5 cm are placed in an empty rectangular tank measuring 20 cm by 20 cm by 11 cm. The tank is then filled with water flowing from a tap at a rate of 6 litres per minute. How long will it take to fill up the tank? (1 litre = 1000 cm³)

Volume of 4 metal cubes = 5 × 5 × 5 × 4
= 500 cm³

Volume of tank = 20 × 20 × 11
= 4400 cm³

Volume of water = 4400 − 500
= 3900 cm³
= 3.9 ℓ

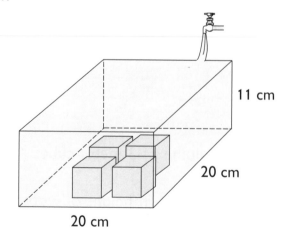

Time taken $= \dfrac{3.9}{6}$

= ■ min

Workbook Exercise 15

PRACTICE 3A

1. The volume of a cube is 216 cm³. Find the area of one face of the cube.

2. The volume of a box is 3600 cm³. Its breadth is 15 cm. Its length is twice its breadth. Find its height.

3. Find the unknown edge of each cuboid.

(a)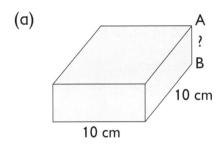

Volume = 400 cm³
AB = ■ cm

(b)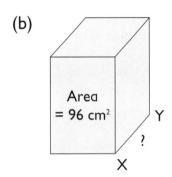

Volume = 768 cm³
XY = ■ cm

4. The figure shows a cuboid consisting of 12 cubes.
   The area of the shaded face is 36 cm².
   (a) Find the volume of each cube.
   (b) Find the volume of the cuboid.

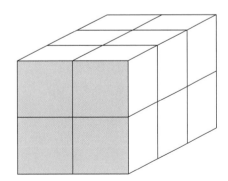

5. The figure shows a solid that is made up of 4 cubes of edge 2 cm.
   (a) Find the volume of the solid.
   (b) If the solid is painted red, find the total area which is painted red.

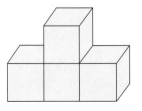

PRACTICE 3B

1. The base of a rectangular tank measures 50 cm by 40 cm. What will be the height of the water level when it contains 9 litres of water?
(1 litre = 1000 cm^3)

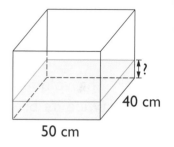

2. A rectangular tank measuring 18 m by 18 m by 6 m is $\frac{2}{3}$ filled with water. If the water is poured into another rectangular tank which is 12 m long and 10 m wide, what will be the height of the water level in the second tank?

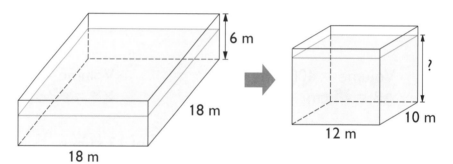

3. An empty rectangular tank measures 60 cm by 50 cm by 56 cm. It is being filled with water flowing from a tap at a rate of 8 litres per minute.
   (a) Find the capacity of the tank.
   (b) How long will it take to fill up the tank?
   (1 litre = 1000 cm^3)

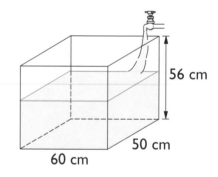

4. The base of a rectangular tank measures 50 cm by 40 cm. It contains 60 litres of water when it is $\frac{3}{4}$ full. Find the height of the tank. (1 litre = 1000 cm^3)

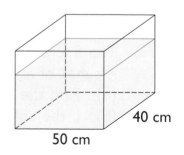

44

PRACTICE 3C

1. A rectangular tank, 25 cm long and 25 cm wide, is filled with water to a depth of 10 cm. When a metal cube of edge 10 cm is placed in the tank, the water level rises. Find the height of the new water level.

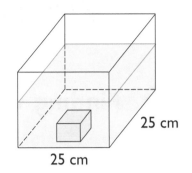

2. A rectangular tank measuring 50 cm by 50 cm by 42 cm was $\frac{2}{3}$ filled with water. When a stone was placed in the tank, the tank became $\frac{3}{4}$ full.

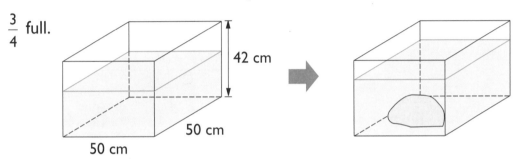

   (a) Find the capacity of the tank in cubic centimetres.
   (b) Find the volume of the stone.

3. An empty rectangular tank measures 70 cm by 25 cm by 36 cm. A stone of volume 4500 cm³ is placed in the tank. Then the tank is filled with water flowing from a tap at a rate of 9 litres per minute. How long will it take to fill up the tank?
   (1 litre = 1000 cm³)

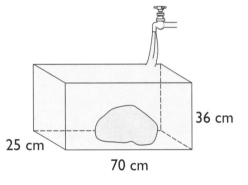

*4. Ali placed a stone in an empty rectangular tank, 50 cm long and 40 cm wide. He then filled the tank with water flowing from a tap at a rate of 10 litres per minute. It took 3 minutes to fill the tank to a depth of 18 cm to cover the stone completely. Find the volume of the stone.
   (1 litre = 1000 cm³)

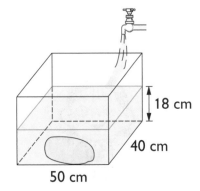

45

4 Triangles and 4-sided Figures

1 Finding Unknown Angles

In the figure, ABCE is a parallelogram, CDE is an equilateral triangle and BCD is a straight line.

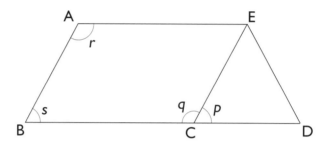

$\angle p = \blacksquare°$

$\angle q = \blacksquare°$

$\angle r = \blacksquare°$

$\angle s = \blacksquare°$

CDE is an equilateral triangle.
What can you say about its angles?

ABCE is a parallelogram.
What can you say about its angles?

ABDE is a trapezium.
What can you say about its angles?

1. In the figure, XW = XY, ∠WXY = 38° and XYZ is a straight line. Find ∠XWY and ∠WYZ.

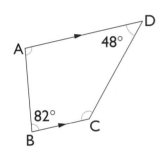

∠XWY = (180° − 38°) ÷ 2

= ■°

∠WYZ = ■°

2. In trapezium ABCD, AD // BC, ∠ABC = 82° and ∠ADC = 48°. Find ∠BAD and ∠BCD.

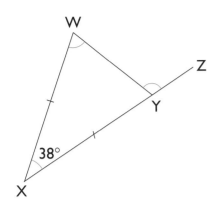

Each pair of angles between two parallel sides add up to 180°.

∠BAD = 180° − 82° = ■°

∠BCD = 180° − 48° = ■°

3. In rhombus WXYZ, ∠WXY = 84°. Find ∠WZY and ∠XWY.

A rhombus has 4 equal sides.

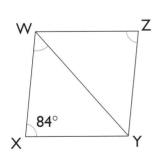

∠WZY = ■°

∠XWY = ■°

Workbook Exercise 16

4. In the figure, WXYZ is a parallelogram, ZV = ZW, ∠ZVW = 52°
   and VWX is a straight line. Find ∠XYZ.

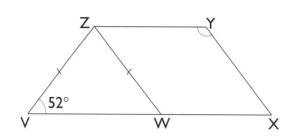

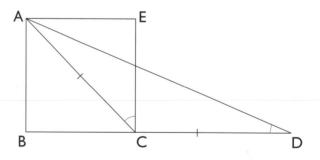

∠ZWV = ◼°

∠ZWX = ◼°

∠XYZ = ◼°

5. In the figure, ABCE is a square, AC = CD and BCD is a straight line.
   Find ∠ACE and ∠CDA.

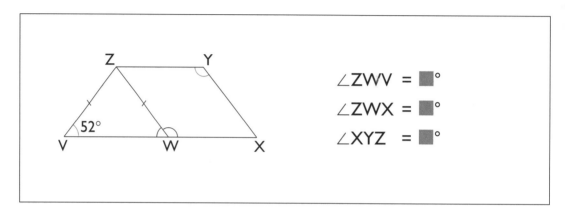

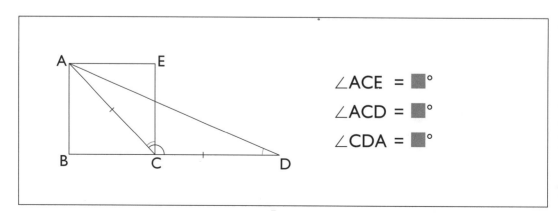

∠ACE = ◼°

∠ACD = ◼°

∠CDA = ◼°

48

6. In the figure, PQRT is a parallelogram, QR = RS, ∠TRS = 90° and ∠QPT = 62°. Find ∠RSQ.

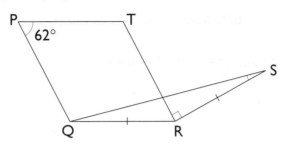

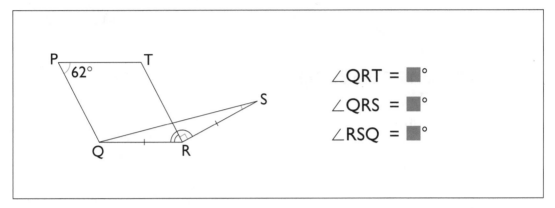

∠QRT = ■°

∠QRS = ■°

∠RSQ = ■°

7. In the figure, ABCD is a rhombus, BE = BC and ∠CBE = 50°. Find ∠DCE.

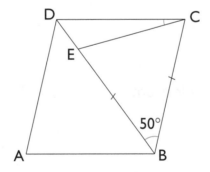

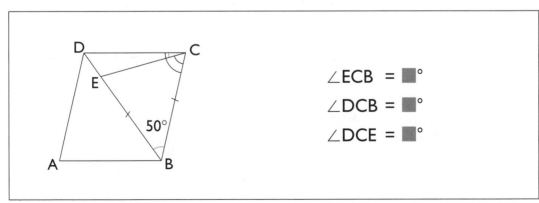

∠ECB = ■°

∠DCB = ■°

∠DCE = ■°

Workbook Exercise 17

49

PRACTICE 4A

The following figures are not drawn to scale.

1. XPY and XQZ are straight lines.
    PQ // YZ
    Find ∠a and ∠b.

    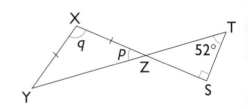

2. XZS and YZT are straight lines.
    XY = XZ
    Find ∠p and ∠q.

    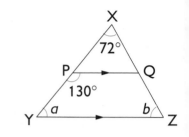

3. ABC is a right-angled triangle.
    BCD is an isosceles triangle.
    BC = BD
    Find ∠x.

    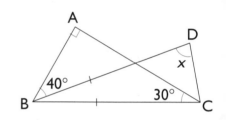

4. PQRS is a parallelogram.
    PQ = TQ
    Find ∠m.

    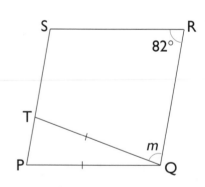

5. EFGH is a parallelogram.
    FG = FH
    Find ∠h.

    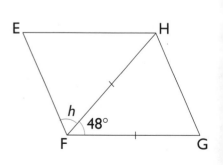

PRACTICE 4B

The following figures are not drawn to scale.

1. MKL is an equilateral triangle.
    IM // JL
    Find ∠p and ∠q.

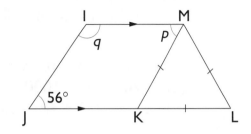

2. ABCD is a parallelogram.
    CDE is a straight line.
    Find ∠a and ∠b.

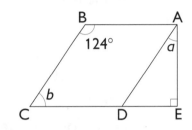

3. UWX and VWZ are straight lines.
    VW = UW
    WZ // XY
    Find ∠x and ∠y.

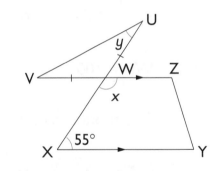

4. FGHI is a rectangle.
    IJHK is a rhombus.
    Find ∠m.

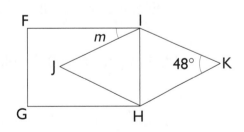

5. PQRS is a square.
    RST is an isosceles triangle.
    RS = ST
    Find ∠w.

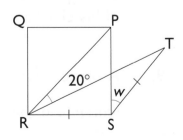

REVIEW C

1. Write the following in figures.
   (a) Thirty thousand and thirty
   (b) Three million and forty thousand

2. What is the missing number in each ■?
   (a) $6205 = 6 \times 1000 + 2 \times ■ + 5$
   (b) $2.098 = 2 + ■ + 0.008$

3. What is the number indicated by the arrow?

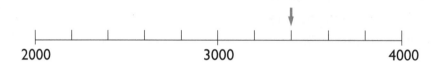

4. Which one of the following is the best estimate of the value of $3594 \div 597$?

   6,   0.6,   0.06,   0.006

5. Write $100 \div 3$ as a mixed number.

6. The table shows the rates of charges for printing T-shirts.

First 50 T-shirts	$9 each
Every additional T-shirt	$8

   Mr Lin printed 80 T-shirts. How much did he have to pay?

7. Mr Lin gave $\frac{1}{3}$ of his money to his wife. He divided the remainder equally between his 3 children. What fraction of his money did each of his children receive?

8. A container is $\frac{2}{3}$ full when it contains 60 litres of water. How much water is in the container when it is $\frac{3}{5}$ full?

9. Express 24 : 6 : 15 in its simplest form.

10. $\frac{1}{3}$ of John's savings is twice as much as David's savings. Find the ratio of John's savings to David's savings.

11. The ratio of John's money to Peter's money is 3 : 5. Express Peter's money as a fraction of John's money.

12. John spent $32 and had $48 left. What percentage of his money did he spend?

13. $\frac{1}{4}$ of a circle is coloured blue. 20% of the remainder is coloured red. What percentage of the circle is coloured red?

14. The pie chart shows how a group of pupils travel to school.
What percentage of the pupils walk to school?

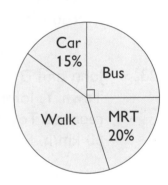

15. Express 2.5% as a fraction in its simplest form.

16. Find the value of 20% of $14.50.

17. Mr Lin started jogging at 6.30 a.m. By 8.30 a.m., he had jogged a distance of 8 km. Find his average speed in km/h.

18. Mr Chen earns 3¢ from every newspaper he delivers. He earns an extra $3 for every 400 newspapers delivered. How much will he earn if he delivers 2000 newspapers?

19. A tank was $\frac{2}{5}$ filled with water. After another 36 litres of water were poured in, the tank became $\frac{2}{3}$ full. Find the capacity of the tank.

20. The ratio of the number of blue beads to the number of red beads in a jar was 2 : 5 at first. Ali removed $\frac{1}{4}$ of the blue beads and $\frac{2}{5}$ of the red beads from the jar.
   (a) Find the new ratio of the number of blue beads to the number of red beads.
   (b) If there were 12 more red beads than blue beads left in the jar, how many beads were removed altogether?

21. The breadth of a rectangle is $\frac{2}{3}$ of its length. If the perimeter of the rectangle is 40 cm, find the area of the rectangle.

22. Mr Wu took $1\frac{1}{2}$ hours to cover $\frac{2}{3}$ of a journey. He took $\frac{1}{2}$ hour to cover the remaining journey at an average speed of 72 km/h. Find his average speed for the whole journey.

23. John and David both drove a distance of 80 km from Town X to Town Y. John left Town X 20 minutes earlier than David. They reached Town Y at the same time. If John's average speed was 60 km/h, find David's average speed.

24. Simplify $9t - 6t + t - 2$.

25. Mrs Li bought 3 bottles of shampoo at $\$n$ each and 5 tubes of toothpaste at $\$2$ each. She gave the cashier $\$50$. How much change did she receive? Give your answer in terms of n.

26. In the figure, not drawn to scale, find $\angle x$.

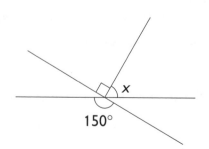

150°

27. In the figure, not drawn to scale, PQ = PR = RS. QRS is a straight line. Find ∠RPS.

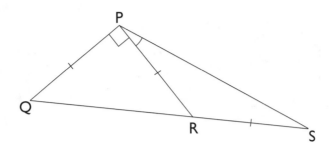

28. In the figure, ABCD is a parallelogram. Find ∠x.

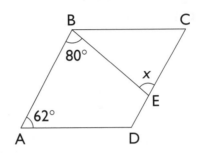

29. Find the shaded area in the rectangle.

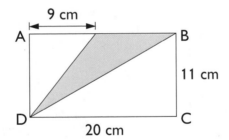

30. The figure shows three semicircular shapes of the same size. Find its area in terms of π.

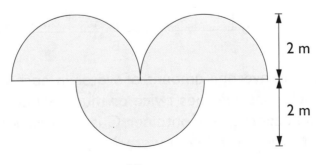

31. Cuboid A has the same volume as Cuboid B. Find the height of Cuboid B.

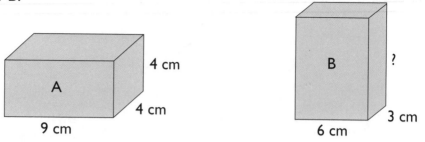

32. A rectangular tank, measuring 40 cm by 30 cm by 30 cm, is $\frac{1}{2}$ filled with water. If the water is drained out at a rate of 10 litres per minute, how long will it take to empty the water from the tank? (1 litre = 1000 cm³)

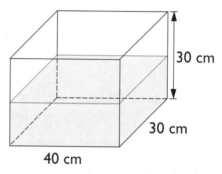

33. The bar graph shows the amounts of water in 5 containers, A, B, C, D and E.

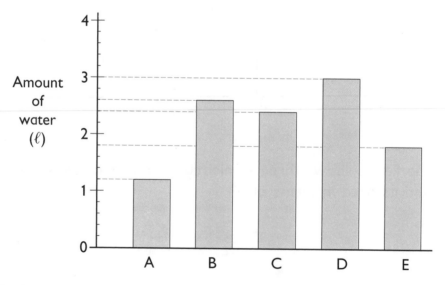

(a) Find the average amount of water in each container.
(b) Which container has twice as much water as Container A?
(c) If the capacity of Container C is 4 litres, what fraction of the container is filled with water?

REVIEW D

1. What is the missing number in each ■?
   (a) $80\ 609 = 80\ 000 + ■ + 9$
   (b) $6.708 = 6 + \dfrac{7}{10} + \dfrac{8}{■}$

2. Find the value of each of the following:
   (a) $(84 - 4 \times 15) \div 3$ (b) $7 \times 8 - 42 \div 7$

3. Find the value of $478 \div 36$ correct to 2 decimal places.

4. Express each of the following as a decimal.
   (a) $\dfrac{3}{8}$ (b) 82%

5. Which one of the following fractions is the smallest?
   $$\dfrac{3}{15}, \quad \dfrac{3}{7}, \quad \dfrac{3}{4}, \quad \dfrac{2}{5}$$

6. Find the value of $\dfrac{1}{3} \times 4.2$.

7. A bus took 4 hours and 35 minutes to travel from Town A to Town B. It reached Town B at 2.00 p.m. What time did it leave Town A?

8. Express each of the following as a fraction in its simplest form.
   (a) 8%   (b) 4.28

9. Express each of the following as a percentage.
   (a) $\dfrac{8}{25}$ (b) 0.45

10. What fraction of 2 kg is 275 g? Give your answer in its simplest form.

11. Express $1.80 as a percentage of $5.

12. What is the missing number in each ■?
    (a) $\dfrac{5}{8} = ■ : 8$ (b) $2 : 3 : 5 = ■ : 9 : ■$

13. Mr Li bought 15 oranges at 3 for $1. How much did he pay?

14. Jim and David have $603 altogether. Jim has $115 more than David. How much money does David have?

15. There are 144 people in a hall. 56 of them are women. The rest are men. What fraction of the people in the hall are men?

16. Annie and Betty shared $\frac{1}{2}$ of a pizza. Betty received twice as much as Annie. What fraction of a whole pizza did Betty receive?

17. Mrs Lin bought $\frac{1}{2}$ kg of prawns at $0.90 per 100 g. How much did she pay?

18. Meihua spent 15% of her money on a music box. If the music box cost $60, how much had she left?

19. During a sale, a shop reduced the prices of all its watches by 30%.
    (a) If the usual price of a watch was $55, find its sale price.
    (b) If the sale price of a watch was $42, find its usual price.

20. Muthu is cycling at a speed of 200 m/min. How long will he take to cycle 1 km?

21. Mr Lin had 240 apples and pears. After selling 82 apples and 26 pears, he had 3 times as many apples as pears left. How many apples did he have at first?

22. Alan, Dave and Linda shared 600 stamps. Dave received twice as many stamps as Alan. Linda received 40 more stamps than Alan. How many stamps did Alan receive?

23. John and Mary had $350 altogether. After John spent $\frac{1}{2}$ of his money and Mary spent $\frac{1}{3}$ of her money, they each had an equal amount of money left. How much did they spend altogether?

24. Mrs Wang had 84 tarts. 24 of them were cherry tarts. The rest were pineapple tarts and apple tarts. There were 18 more pineapple tarts than cherry tarts. Find the ratio of the number of pineapple tarts to the number of cherry tarts to the number of apple tarts.

25. Mrs Lin had goldfish and angelfish for sale. She sold $\frac{3}{4}$ of the goldfish and $\frac{1}{2}$ of the angelfish. If she had 20 goldfish and 30 angelfish left, how many fish did Mrs Lin have altogether at first?

26. The ratio of Tom's money to Dick's money to Harry's money is 3 : 2 : 4. If Dick gives $\frac{1}{4}$ of his money to Harry, what will be the new ratio of Tom's money to Dick's money to Harry's money?

27. The ratio of Ali's money to Rahim's money was 3 : 2. After Ali gave Rahim $15, Ali still had $10 more than Rahim. How much money did Ali have at first?

28. Mrs Chen used 40% of a packet of flour to bake cakes. She used 35% of the remainder to make pizzas. What percentage of the packet of flour did she use to make pizzas?

29. Halim and Jimmy cycled from Town A to Town B at 15 km/h and 12 km/h respectively. They both started from Town A at 10.00 a.m. If Jimmy reached Town B at 10.30 a.m., what time did Halim reach Town B?

30. Peter and David start out on a 10-km walk at the same time. When Peter completes the 10 km, David still has 2 km to walk. If Peter's walking speed is 5 km/h, find David's walking speed.

31. Simplify $4a + 6 + 8a - 3 - a$.

32. The figure is made up of a semicircle, a square and a triangle. Find its area. (Take $\pi = 3.14$)

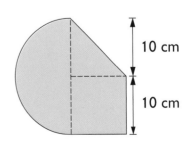

10 cm

10 cm

33. Tank A has a square base of area 36 cm² and its height is 8 cm. It is completely filled with water. Tank B is empty and it measures 5 cm by 3 cm by 12 cm. The water in Tank A is poured into Tank B to fill it to its brim. Find the height of the new water level in Tank A.

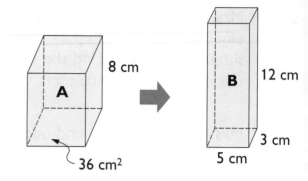

34. In the figure, not drawn to scale, ACE and BCD are straight lines. Find ∠CDE.

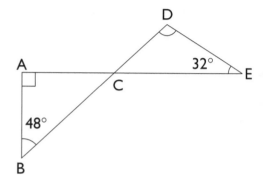

35. Which solid can be formed by the given net?

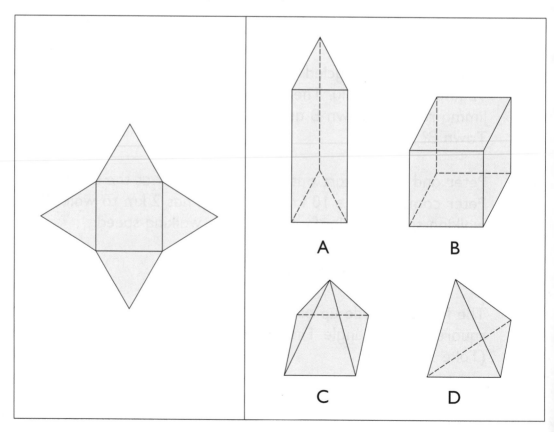

36. The figure shows half of a symmetric figure which has the dotted line as a line of symmetry. Copy and complete the symmetric figure on dotted paper.

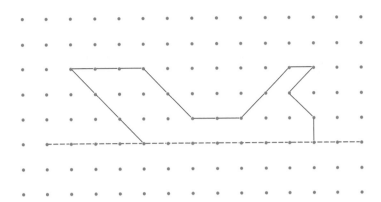

37. The line graph shows the amount of petrol used by Mr Lin in the first six months of a year.

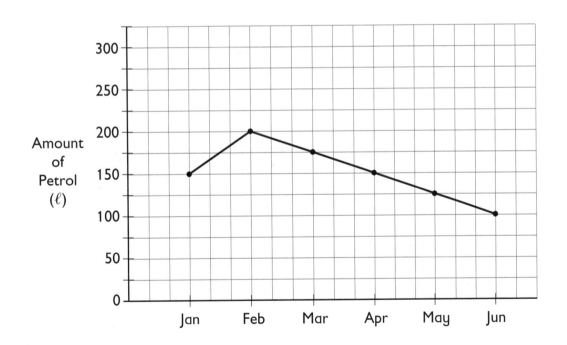

(a) What was the increase in the amount of petrol used from January to February?

(b) What was the average amount of petrol used per month?

(c) If petrol cost $1.15 per litre, how much did Mr Lin spend on petrol in February?

REVIEW E

1. Find the value of 2400 ÷ 3000.

2. Find the value of 6.5 × 4000.

3. Which one of the following is the best estimate of the value of 796.8 ÷ 19.2?

   4,   40,   400,   4000

4. The figure shows part of a weighing scale.

   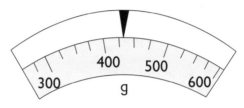

   Which one of the following is closest to the reading indicated by the arrow?

   410 g,   420 g,   430 g,   450 g

5. What fraction of the figure is shaded? Give your answer in its simplest form.

   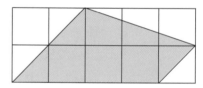

6. Which one of the following fractions is the smallest?

   $\dfrac{5}{3}$, $\dfrac{4}{5}$, $\dfrac{9}{10}$, $1\dfrac{1}{2}$

7. Which one of the following is the same as $\dfrac{2}{25}$?

   0.02,   0.08,   0.2,   0.8

8. Express 2.08 as a mixed number in its simplest form.

9. Arrange the lengths in increasing order.

   2 m,   2.6 m,   2.49 m, $2\dfrac{1}{4}$ m

10. Express 45 minutes out of 2 hours as a fraction in its simplest form.

11. The capacity of a cup is $\frac{1}{4}$ litre. How many cups of water will make up 2 litres?

12. Lihua had 45 oranges. She sold all of them at 3 for $2. How much money did she receive?

13. Siti bought 3 kg of prawns and 3 kg of mutton. She spent a total of $46.50. If 1 kg of prawns cost $9, find the cost of 1 kg of mutton.

14. Mrs Lin can type 225 words in 5 minutes. At this rate, if she types from 10.30 a.m. to 11.15 a.m., how many words will she type?

15. If $\frac{2}{3}$ of a number is 12, what is the value of $\frac{1}{2}$ of the number?

16. Mrs Wu bought some cup cakes. She put $\frac{2}{5}$ of them on a tray and the rest in a box. If there were 8 cup cakes on the tray, how many cup cakes were there in the box?

17. 10 glasses of water can fill $\frac{5}{8}$ of a bottle. How many **more** glasses of water are needed to fill up the bottle?

18. There are 40 children in a class. 24 of them are boys. What is the ratio of the number of boys to the number of girls?

19. The average weight of a man and a boy is 60 kg. If the boy weighs $\frac{2}{3}$ as much as the man, what is the weight of the boy?

20. Devi, Siti and Meiling shared a sum of money in the ratio 5 : 3 : 4. If Devi received $24 more than Siti, how much money did Meiling receive?

21. Cik Siti made 800 cookies. She sold 750 of them. What percentage of the cookies had she left?

22. There are 120 pupils in a school band. 45% of them are girls. How many more boys than girls are there?

23. There are 1800 pupils in a school. This number is 20% more than what it was last year. Find the number of pupils in the school last year.

24. A train took 45 minutes to travel from Town A to Town B. The average speed for the journey was 80 km/h. Find the distance between the two towns.

25. Gopal had 140 stamps and Samy had 100 stamps. After Samy gave Gopal some stamps, Gopal had 3 times as many stamps as Samy. How many stamps did Samy give Gopal?

26. Meihua paid $4.70 for 3 mangoes and 4 apples. If a mango cost 40¢ more than an apple, find the cost of a mango.

27. Liling paid $19.50 for three books, A, B and C. Book A cost $5 more than Book B. Book B cost $2 more than Book C. Find the cost of Book C.

28. Mr Lin spent an average of $250 per month from January to March. He spent an average of $300 per month in April and May. Find the average amount of money Mr Lin spent per month during the 5 months.

29. Mr Chen bought 20 watches for $500. He sold $\frac{3}{4}$ of them at $40 each. He sold the rest at cost price. How much money did he make?

30. When a bottle is $\frac{1}{2}$ filled with water, it weighs 2.6 kg. The bottle weighs 4 kg when it is full. Find the weight of the empty bottle.

31. Mary's savings is $\frac{5}{8}$ of Devi's savings. What is the ratio of Mary's savings to Devi's savings?

32. Rahim has 30% more books than Gopal. If Rahim has 65 books, how many books does Gopal have?

33. Siti sold x tarts on Monday. She sold 3 times as many tarts on Tuesday as on Monday. She sold 36 more tarts on Wednesday than on Monday. Find the total number of tarts she sold in the three days. Give your answer in terms of x in its simplest form.

34. The area of a square is half the area of the rectangle. Find the perimeter of the square.

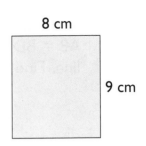

8 cm

9 cm

35. Find the shaded area in the rectangle.

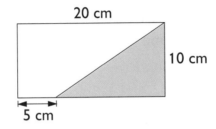

20 cm

10 cm

5 cm

36. The cardboard is in a shape of a semicircle and a quarter circle. Find its perimeter. (Take π = 3.14)

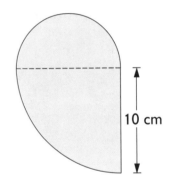

10 cm

37. The solid is made up of 3 cubes of the same size. If the area of the shaded face is 16 cm^2, find the volume of the solid.

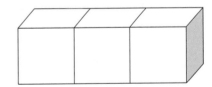

38. The base of a container is a square of side 30 cm. A stone is placed in the container. Then water is poured into the container until it is $\frac{3}{4}$ full.

When the stone is removed, the water level drops to $\frac{5}{8}$ of the height of the container.

If the volume of the stone is 4500 cm^3, find the height of the container.

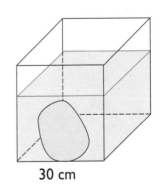

30 cm

65

39. In the figure, not drawn to scale, AB = BD = CD. ABC is a straight line. Find ∠BAD.

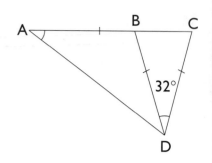

40. In the figure, not drawn to scale, AD // BC and ABC is an equilateral triangle. Find ∠x.

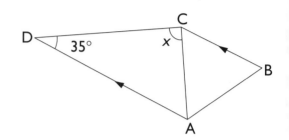

41. How many faces does the solid have?

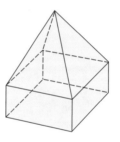

42. The pie chart represents the number of people on a cruise.

$\frac{1}{8}$ of the people were girls.

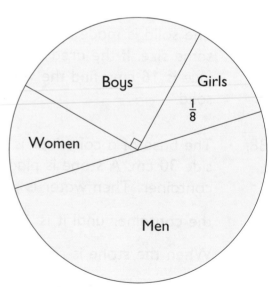

(a) What fraction of the people were boys?
(b) What fraction of the people were women?
(c) There were 120 girls on the cruise. How many people were there altogether?

5 *More Challenging Word Problems

1 Whole Numbers and Decimals

1. Raju had 3 times as much money as Gopal. After Raju spent $60 and Gopal spent $10, they each had an equal amount of money left. How much money did Raju have at first?

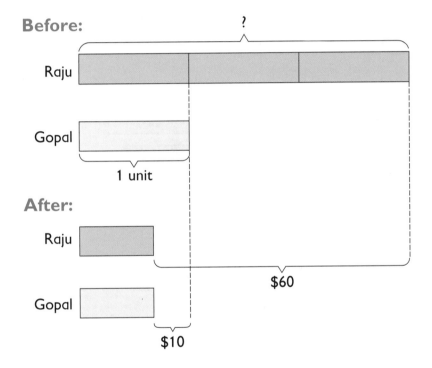

2 units = $60 − $10 = $50

1 unit = $50 ÷ 2 = $25

Raju's money at first = 3 units

$$= \$25 \times 3$$

$$= \$75$$

2. Ali had $130 and his brother had $45. When their mother gave each of them an equal amount of money, Ali had twice as much money as his brother. How much money did their mother give each of them?

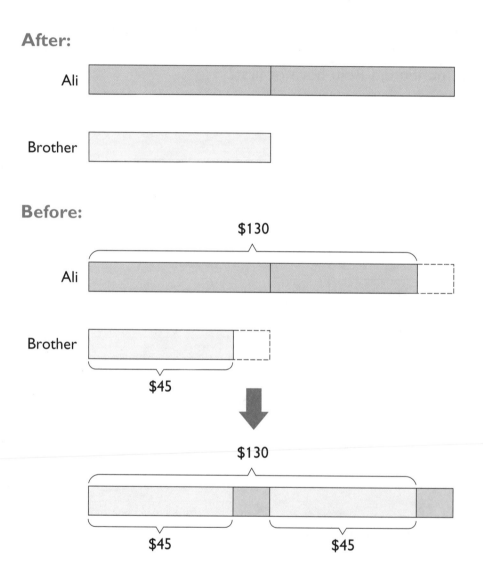

$130 − $45 − $45 = $40

Their mother gave each of them $40.

3. Sulin is given $5 more pocket money than Meihua each week. They each spend $12 per week and save the rest. When Sulin saves $60, Meihua saves $20. How much pocket money does each girl have per week?

Pocket money per week:

Sulin saves $5 more than Meihua each week.

Total savings:

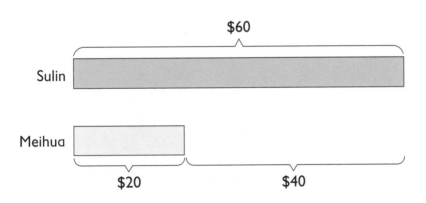

Difference in savings = $60 − $20 = $40

40 ÷ 5 = 8

They take 8 weeks to save the given amounts of money.

Sulin's savings per week = $60 ÷ 8 = $7.50

Sulin's pocket money per week = $7.50 + $12 = $19.50

Meihua's pocket money per week = $19.50 − $5 = $14.50

4.   The average weight of Henry, Peter and John is 35.5 kg. Peter is twice as heavy as John. Henry is 4 kg lighter than Peter. Find Peter's weight.

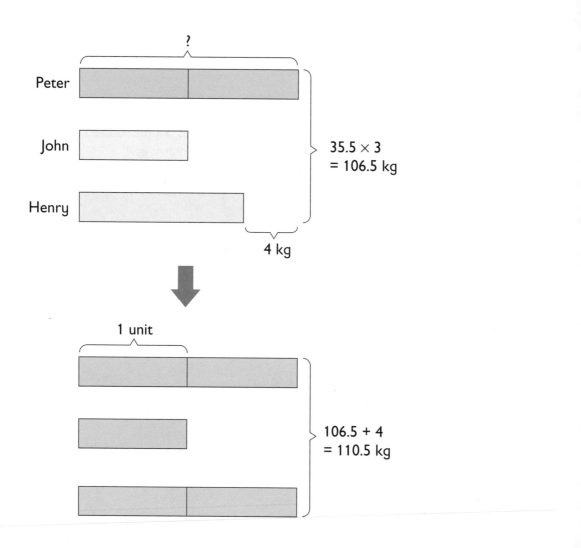

5 units = 110.5 kg

1 unit = 110.5 ÷ 5

        = 22.1 kg

Peter's weight = 2 units

              = 22.1 × 2

              = 44.2 kg

PRACTICE 5A

1. There are 148 more blue beads than green beads in a box. If another 12 blue beads and 28 green beads are put into the box, how many more blue beads than green beads will there be in the box?

2. Mrs Lin bought 600 g of prawns and 40 fishballs for $18. If 10 fishballs cost $1.50, find the cost of 1 kg of prawns.

3. Meihua bought 100 mangoes for $90. She threw away 16 rotten ones and sold the rest at 3 for $4. How much money did she make?

4. A racket and 4 shuttlecocks cost $13.75. The racket costs $5.50 more than each shuttlecock. Find the cost of the racket.

5. Rosnah had 3 times as much money as Minah. After Rosnah spent $9 and Minah was given $5, they each had an equal amount of money. How much money did Rosnah have at first?

6. Mrs Chen has a bag of sweets for her class. If she gives each pupil 8 sweets, she will have 4 sweets left. If she gives only 5 sweets to each pupil, she will have 40 sweets left. How many pupils are there in the class?

7. Minghua and Fuming had $30 and $75 respectively. After they each received an equal amount of money, Fuming had twice as much money as Minghua. How much money did each boy receive?

8. John had 35 more stickers than Tom. After Tom gave John 15 stickers, John had twice as many stickers as Tom. How many stickers did they have altogether?

9. Rahim and Ahmad each had an equal amount of money. Each day Rahim spent $18 and Ahmad spent $24. When Ahmad used up all his money, Rahim still had $120 left. How much money did each of them have at first?

10. There were twice as many carnations as roses in a flower shop. After selling 50 carnations and 10 roses, there were 3 times as many roses as carnations left in the shop. How many roses were there in the shop at first?

2 Fractions

1. $\frac{3}{5}$ of the beads in a box are yellow beads. The rest are red beads and blue beads. There are twice as many yellow beads as red beads. There are 30 more red beads than blue beads. Find the total number of yellow beads and red beads.

Method 1:

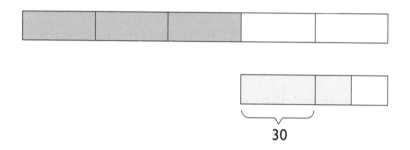

Number of yellow beads = 30 × 3

= 90

Number of red beads = 90 ÷ 2

= 45

Total number of yellow beads and red beads

= 90 + 45 = 135

Method 2:

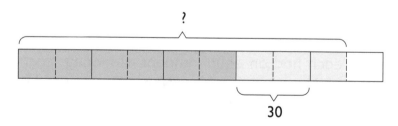

2 units = 30

1 unit = 30 ÷ 2 = 15

Total number of yellow beads and red beads

= 9 units = 15 × 9 = 135

2. $\frac{1}{4}$ of the beads in a box are red. There are 24 more yellow beads than red beads. The remaining 76 beads are blue. How many beads are there altogether?

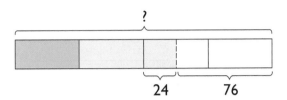

$\frac{1}{2}$ ——→ 24 + 76 = 100 beads

1 ——→ 200 beads

There are 200 beads altogether.

3. 10 jugs of water can fill $\frac{5}{8}$ of a pail. Another 4 jugs and 5 cups of water are needed to fill the remaining part of the pail. How many cups of water can the pail hold?

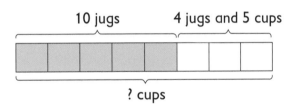

$\frac{5}{8}$ ——→ 10 jugs

$\frac{1}{8}$ ——→ 2 jugs

$\frac{2}{8}$ ——→ 4 jugs

$\frac{1}{8}$ ——→ 5 cups

1 ——→ 40 cups

The pail can hold 40 cups of water.

4. Meihua spent $\frac{1}{3}$ of her money on a book. She spent $\frac{3}{4}$ of the remainder on a pen. If the pen cost $6 more than the book, how much money did she spend altogether?

Method 1:

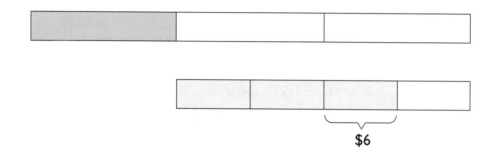

$6

Cost of pen = $6 × 3

$\qquad$ = $18

Cost of book = $18 − $6

$\qquad$ = $12

Total amount of money spent = $18 + $12

$\qquad$ = $30

Method 2:

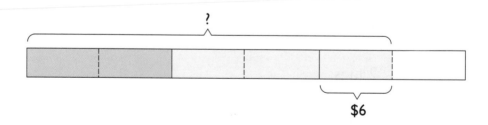

?

$6

1 unit = $6

Total amount of money spent = 5 units

$\qquad$ = $6 × 5

$\qquad$ = $30

5. Henry bought 280 blue and red paper cups. He used $\frac{1}{3}$ of the blue ones and $\frac{1}{2}$ of the red ones at a party. If he had an equal number of blue cups and red cups left, how many cups did he use altogether?

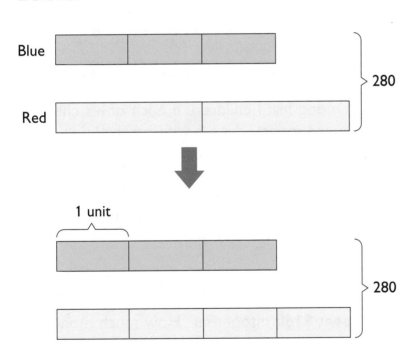

7 units = 280

1 unit = 280 ÷ 7

= 40

Total number of cups used = 3 units

= 40 × 3

= 120

PRACTICE 5B

1. Meilin spent $\frac{3}{4}$ of her money on a dictionary. She spent $\frac{1}{2}$ of the remainder on a calculator. The dictionary cost $30 more than the calculator. How much did the dictionary cost?

2. Rahman bought a pen with $\frac{2}{5}$ of his money. Then he bought a jacket which cost $5 more than the pen. He spent $105 altogether. How much money had he left?

3. Mrs Wu spends $\frac{3}{5}$ of her money on 3 bowls and 8 plates. With the rest of her money, she can buy another 6 bowls. If she spends all her money on plates only, how many plates can she buy?

4. Mr Lin gave $\frac{3}{5}$ of a sum of money to his wife. Then he divided the remainder equally among his 4 children. If each of his children received $80, how much money did his wife receive?

5. Susan bought some towels. $\frac{2}{5}$ of them were pink and $\frac{1}{4}$ of them were blue. The remaining 28 towels were white. How many more pink towels than blue towels did she buy?

6. Samy spent $\frac{1}{3}$ of his money in the first week and $\frac{1}{5}$ of it in the second week. He spent $160 altogether. How much money did he have at first?

7. Mingfa spent $\frac{1}{4}$ of his money on a toy car. He spent $\frac{1}{2}$ of the remainder on a calculator. He had $18 left. How much did he spend altogether?

8. Rahman spent $\frac{3}{4}$ of his money on 3 mangoes and 6 apples. If a mango cost 3 times as much as an apple, how many apples could he buy with the rest of his money?

PRACTICE 5C

1. Aihua bought a bag of beads. $\frac{1}{3}$ of the beads were green, $\frac{1}{9}$ were black and $\frac{1}{5}$ of the remainder were white. If there were 25 white beads, how many beads were there altogether?

2. Huaming spent $\frac{3}{5}$ of his money on a watch. He spent $\frac{1}{4}$ of the remainder on a calculator. The watch cost $28 more than the calculator. How much money did he have at first?

3. Mr Wu spent $\frac{3}{5}$ of a sum of money on a dining table. He used the rest of the money to buy 6 chairs. If each chair cost $25, find the cost of the table.

4. $\frac{3}{5}$ of Mary's flowers were roses and the rest were orchids. After giving away $\frac{1}{2}$ of the roses and $\frac{1}{4}$ of the orchids, she had 54 flowers left. How many flowers did she have at first?

5. A bottle weighs 1.5 kg when it is $\frac{1}{5}$ filled with cooking oil. It weighs 3.3 kg when it is $\frac{4}{5}$ full. Find the weight of the empty bottle.

6. Meiling and Fumin had $280 altogether. After Meiling spent $\frac{1}{2}$ of her money and Fumin spent $\frac{1}{4}$ of his money, they each had the same amount of money left. How much money did Meiling have at first?

7. Lihui spent $\frac{2}{5}$ of his money on a storybook and a magazine. The storybook cost 3 times as much as the magazine. If he had $24 left, find the cost of the storybook.

8. Meiling spent an equal amount of money each day. After 4 days, she had $\frac{4}{5}$ of her money left. After another 10 days, she had $30 left. How much money did she have at first?

77

3 Ratio

1. $\frac{2}{5}$ of the beads in a box are yellow beads. The rest are red beads and blue beads. The ratio of the number of red beads to the number of blue beads is 4 : 5. If there are 30 blue beads, how many yellow beads are there?

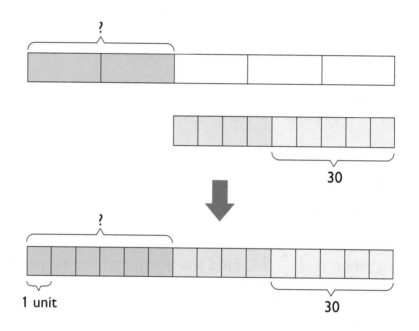

5 units = 30

1 unit = 30 ÷ 5

= 6

Number of yellow beads = 6 units

= 6 × 6

= 36

2. The ratio of Peter's money to John's money was 3 : 5 at first. After Peter's money was increased by $250 and John's money was decreased by $350, they had an equal amount of money each. How much money did Peter have at first?

Before:

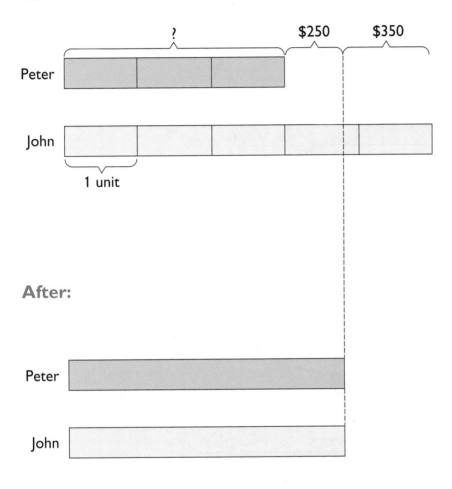

After:

2 units = $250 + $350

       = $600

1 unit = $600 ÷ 2

       = $300

Peter's money at first = 3 units

                    = $300 × 3

                    = $900

3. Susan's money was $\frac{2}{3}$ of Mary's money at first. After Mary gave $\frac{1}{2}$ of her money to Susan, Susan had $175. How much money did Susan have at first?

Before:

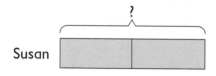

Susan

Mary

After:

$175

Susan

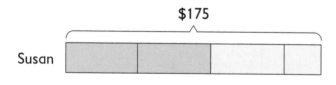

Mary

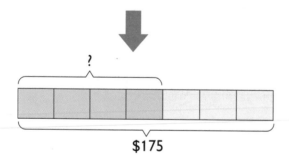

$175

7 units = $175

1 unit = $175 ÷ 7

= $25

Susan's money at first = 4 units

= $25 × 4

= $100

PRACTICE 5D

1. Suhua had $50. Jane had $10 more than Suhua. What was the ratio of Suhua's money to Jane's money?

2. The ratio of the number of girls to the number of boys in an art club is 3 : 5. If there are 18 girls, how many children are there altogether?

3. Peter and Salim shared 360 stamps in the ratio 7 : 5. How many more stamps did Peter receive than Salim?

4. The ratio of the weight of Parcel A to the weight of Parcel B to the weight of Parcel C is 6 : 5 : 3. If Parcel B weighs 420 g, find the total weight of the three parcels.

5. The perimeter of a triangle is 60 cm. If the sides of the triangle are in the ratio 4 : 3 : 5, find the length of the shortest side.

6. Mary, Sufen and Devi shared a sum of money in the ratio 4 : 2 : 5. If Mary received $15 more than Sufen, how much money did Devi receive?

7. The ratio of the number of John's stamps to the number of Peter's stamps is 5 : 8. Peter has 18 more stamps than John. If Peter gives 22 stamps to John, what will be the new ratio of the number of John's stamps to Peter's?

8. The ratio of the number of men to the number of women in a factory is 3 : 8. There are 120 more women than men. If the number of men increases by 3 and the number of women decreases by 12, what will be the new ratio of the number of men to the number of women?

9. Siti's money is $\frac{2}{5}$ of Betty's money. If Betty gives $\frac{1}{2}$ of her money to Siti, what will be the ratio of Siti's money to Betty's money?

10. After Ali gave $\frac{1}{4}$ of his money to Gopal, Gopal had twice as much money as Ali. What was the ratio of Ali's money to Gopal's money at first?

PRACTICE 5E

1. $\frac{1}{3}$ of Carol's age is twice as much as Mary's age. What is the ratio of Carol's age to Mary's age?

2. $\frac{1}{4}$ of Devi's weight is equal to $\frac{2}{5}$ of Gopal's weight. Find the ratio of Devi's weight to Gopal's weight.

3. John has $28 more than Peter. $\frac{1}{3}$ of John's money is equal to $\frac{4}{5}$ of Peter's money. Find John's money.

4. The ratio of the number of boys to the number of girls in a school choir is 2 : 3. $\frac{1}{4}$ of the boys and $\frac{1}{2}$ of the girls wear spectacles. If there are 48 pupils who wear spectacles, how many pupils are there in the choir?

5. The ratio of Kassim's money to Paul's money was 5 : 2 at first. After Kassim gave $30 to Paul, they had an equal amount of money each. How much money did they have altogether?

6. The ratio of the amount of water in a jar to the amount of water in a bottle was 5 : 6. After $\frac{1}{2}$ of the water in the jar was poured into the bottle, the bottle contained 850 ml of water. How much water was there in the bottle at first?

7. The ratio of the number of Sumin's stamps to the number of Meifen's stamps is 5 : 2. Sumin has 42 more stamps than Meifen. How many stamps should Sumin give to Meifen so that the ratio of the number of Sumin's stamps to the number of Meifen's stamps will be 3 : 4?

8. John had $200 and David had $180. After they each spent an equal amount of money, the ratio of John's money to David's money was 3 : 2. How much did each of them spend?

9. The ratio of Sumin's money to Meili's money was 4 : 1. After Sumin spent $26, Sumin had $2 less than Meili. How much money did Sumin have at first?

4 Percentage

1. A shopkeeper had 4 handbags which were of the same cost price. He sold 3 of them at 40% more than the cost price. He sold the fourth handbag at cost price. He received $260 altogether. Find the cost price of each handbag.

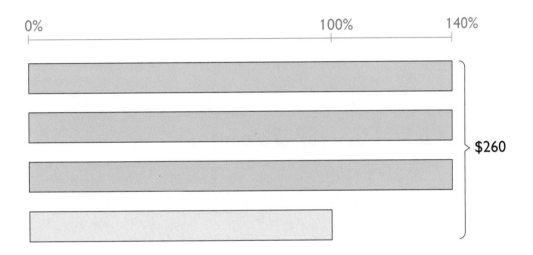

$140 \times 3 + 100 = 520$

$520\% \longrightarrow \$260$

$1\% \longrightarrow \$\dfrac{260}{520}$

$100\% \longrightarrow \$\dfrac{260}{520} \times 100 = \$50$

Cost price of each handbag = $50

2. A club had 600 members. 60% of them were males. When another 200 new members joined the club, the percentage of members who were males was reduced to 50%. How many of the new members were males?

Before:

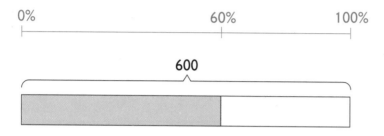

Number of males = 60% of 600 = 360

After:

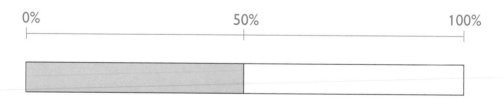

Total number of members = 600 + 200 = 800

Number of males = 50% of 800 = 400

400 − 360 = 40

40 of the new members were males.

PRACTICE 5F

1. 60% of the participants in a road race were males. There were 100 more male than female participants. How many participants took part in the road race?

2. Kumar spent 20% of his savings on a bicycle and 15% of the remainder on a book. What percentage of his savings had he left?

3. There are 5% more boys than girls in an art club. If there are 2 more boys than girls, how many children are there altogether?

4. Last year, Jane gave away 160 balloons to the children at a carnival. This year, she gave away 240 balloons. How many per cent more balloons did she give away this year than last year?

5. Anne bought 72 stamps. She bought 27 more stamps than Betty. How many per cent more stamps did Anne buy than Betty?

6. Mingfa has 420 stamps. 150 of them are Malaysian stamps and the rest are Singapore stamps. How many per cent more Singapore stamps than Malaysian stamps does Mingfa have?

7. Hassan gave 60% of a sum of money to his wife and 25% of the remainder to his mother. He still had $240 left. How much was the sum of money?

8. Jenny and Marvin have 836 stamps altogether. Jenny has 20% more stamps than Marvin. How many more stamps does Jenny have than Marvin?

9. Ailing spent 20% of her money on a dress. She spent $\frac{2}{5}$ of the remainder on a book. She had $72 left. How much money did she have at first?

10. Mr Chen had two vacuum cleaners which were of the same cost price. He sold one of them at 20% more than the cost price. He sold the other at cost price. If he received a total of $286, how much did he earn?

5 Speed

1. Mr Li and Mr Wang both drove a distance of 120 km from Town X to Town Y. Mr Wang started his journey 30 minutes later than Mr Li. They reached Town Y at the same time. If Mr Wang's average speed was 80 km/h, find Mr Li's average speed.

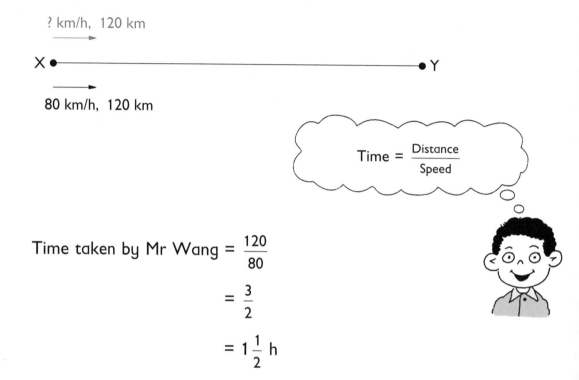

? km/h, 120 km

X •———————————————→• Y

80 km/h, 120 km

Time = $\dfrac{\text{Distance}}{\text{Speed}}$

Time taken by Mr Wang $= \dfrac{120}{80}$

$= \dfrac{3}{2}$

$= 1\dfrac{1}{2}$ h

Mr Li took 30 min more than Mr Wang.

$30 \text{ min} = \dfrac{1}{2}$ h

Time taken by Mr Li $= 1\dfrac{1}{2} + \dfrac{1}{2}$

$= 2$ h

Average speed of Mr Li $= \dfrac{120}{2}$

$= 60$ km/h

2. Mr Raju drove a distance of 80 km from Town A to Town B. He drove at an average speed of 75 km/h for the first 40 minutes. For the rest of the journey, he drove at an average speed of 72 km/h. If he left Town A at 8.30 a.m., what time did he arrive at Town B?

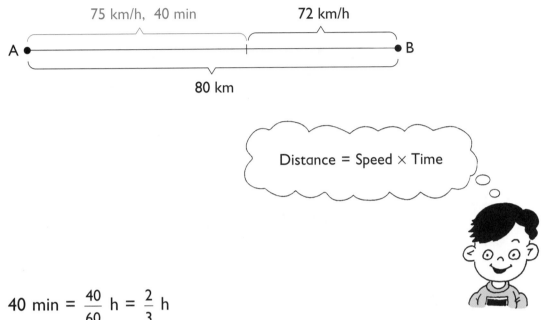

$$40 \text{ min} = \frac{40}{60} \text{ h} = \frac{2}{3} \text{ h}$$

Distance travelled in the 1st part $= 75 \times \frac{2}{3} = 50$ km

Distance travelled in the 2nd part $= 80 - 50 = 30$ km

Time taken for the 2nd part $= \frac{30}{72}$ h

$$= \frac{30}{72} \times 60 \text{ min}$$

$$= 25 \text{ min}$$

Total time taken $= 40 + 25$

$$= 65 \text{ min}$$

$$= 1 \text{ h } 5 \text{ min}$$

1 h 5 min after 8.30 a.m. is 9.35 a.m.

Mr Raju arrived at Town B at 9.35 a.m.

3. Encik Rahman drove from Town P to Town Q. He took 2 hours to cover $\frac{3}{4}$ of the journey at an average speed of 60 km/h. He covered the remaining journey at an average speed of 50 km/h. If he arrived at Town Q at 12.00 noon, what time did he leave Town P?

$\frac{3}{4}$ of the journey = 60 × 2

$\qquad\qquad\qquad$ = 120 km

$\frac{1}{4}$ of the journey = 120 ÷ 3

$\qquad\qquad\qquad$ = 40 km

Time taken for the first $\frac{3}{4}$ of the journey = 2 h

Time taken for the remaining journey = $\frac{40}{50}$

$\qquad\qquad\qquad\qquad\qquad\qquad\quad = \frac{4}{5}$ h

Total time taken = 2 + $\frac{4}{5}$

$\qquad\qquad\quad = 2\frac{4}{5}$ h

$\qquad\qquad\quad$ = 2 h 48 min

2 h 48 min before 12.00 noon is 9.12 a.m.

Encik Rahman left Town P at 9.12 a.m.

88

PRACTICE 5G

1. Siti took 2 hours to drive from Town P to Town Q at an average speed of 70 km/h. On her way back, she drove at an average speed of 80 km/h. If she left Town Q at 3.00 p.m., what time did she reach Town P?

2. A van and a car both travelled a distance of 190 km from Rose Town to Orchid Town. The car left Rose Town 50 minutes after the van, but it arrived at Orchid Town 20 minutes earlier than the van. If the average speed of the van was 60 km/h, find the average speed of the car.

3. Mr Chen drove a distance of 120 km from Town P to Town Q at an average speed of 40 km/h. On his way back, he drove at an average speed of 60 km/h. Find his average speed for the whole journey.

4. Encik Rahman drove a distance of 250 km from Town A to Town B. He left Town A at 9.00 a.m. and arrived at Town B at 1.30 p.m. If his average speed for the first $\frac{3}{5}$ of the journey was 60 km/h, find his average speed for the remaining journey.

5. Mr Lin drove from Town X to Town Y. He took $\frac{1}{2}$ hour to cover $\frac{1}{4}$ of the journey at an average speed of 70 km/h. How long did he take to cover the remaining journey if his average speed for the whole journey was 80 km/h?

6. Mr Gopal drove a distance of 80 km from Town X to Town Y. For the first 40 minutes, he drove at an average speed of 72 km/h. His average speed for the remaining journey was 64 km/h. If he arrived at Town Y at 10.00 a.m., what time did he leave Town X?

7. Two towns, A and B, are 20 km apart. At 12.00 noon, Peter left Town A and cycled towards Town B at 15 km/h. At the same time, Henry left Town B and cycled towards Town A at 12 km/h along the same road. Find the distance between Peter and Henry at 12.40 p.m.

REVIEW F

1. (a) Round off 356 490 to the nearest thousand.
   (b) Round off 4.263 to 1 decimal place.

2. Which one of the following decimals is the smallest?
   0.6,   0.25,   0.948,   0.103

3. Which one of the following fractions is smaller than $\frac{2}{5}$?

   $\frac{7}{10}$, $\frac{4}{9}$, $\frac{3}{8}$, $\frac{5}{7}$

4. Express 0.045 as a fraction in its simplest form.

5. Find the value of $\frac{2}{5} \times 60$.

6. Find the value of $7 - 2\frac{5}{6}$.

7. Find the value of each of the following:

   (a) $20 - (12 - 4) \div 4 \times 2$ (b) $2\frac{3}{4} - 1\frac{4}{5}$

8. What is the missing number in each ■?
   (a) $1.95 \times ■ = 1950$ (b) $38 \div ■ = 0.038$

9. Find the value of 3% of $25.

10. 7 out of 200 pupils failed a Mathematics test. What percentage of the pupils passed the test?

11. Meilin's money is $\frac{4}{5}$ of Sufen's money.

    (a) What is the ratio of Meilin's money to Sufen's money?
    (b) Express Meilin's money as a percentage of Sufen's money.

12. John and Hassan shared a sum of money in the ratio 3 : 5.
    (a) What fraction of the sum of money did John receive?
    (b) Express Hassan's share as a fraction of John's share.

13. Siti paid $70 for a calculator and a watch. If the watch cost 3 times as much as the calculator, find the cost of the watch.

14. Mr Chen donated $5 for every $4 donated by Mr Wang. If they donated $1800 altogether, how much money did Mr Wang donate?

15. Susan can type 3 pages in 45 minutes. At this rate, how long will she take to type 24 pages?

16. If 100 g of fish floss cost $3.20, find the cost of $\frac{1}{2}$ kg of fish floss.

17. The average of two numbers is 56. If one number is 10 more than the other, what is the greater number?

18. Mary was given $\frac{1}{4}$ of a sum of money. The remaining money was shared between Alice and Devi in the ratio 4 : 5. What fraction of the sum of money did Devi receive? Give your answer in its simplest form.

19. The average weight of Raju and Gopal is 34 kg. The ratio of Raju's weight to Gopal's weight is 5 : 3. Find Raju's weight.

20. The ratio of the number of boys to the number of girls in a school band is 5 : 3. If $\frac{1}{2}$ of the boys and $\frac{1}{3}$ of the girls wear spectacles, what fraction of the children wear spectacles?

21. Hassan spent $\frac{2}{5}$ of his money. What percentage of his money had he left?

22. During a sale, the price of a dress was reduced from $40 to $24. By what percentage was the price reduced?

23. There are 20% more boys than girls in a computer club. If there are 44 pupils in the computer club, how many girls are there?

24. Hassan cycled from Town A to Town B at a speed of 12 km/h. He took 3 hours to cover $\frac{2}{3}$ of the journey. Find the distance between the two towns.

*25. A blouse cost $10 and a skirt cost twice as much. Mrs Li bought 2 more blouses than skirts. She spent $80 altogether. How many blouses did she buy?

26. Mr Lin bought a table and 4 chairs. The table cost 3 times as much as each chair. If he spent $175 altogether, how much did he pay for each chair?

27. $\frac{1}{2}$ of Ali's money is equal to $\frac{3}{5}$ of Bala's money. If they have $220 altogether, how much money does Ali have?

28. The ratio of the number of red beads to the number of green beads in a box is 3 : 2. If $\frac{1}{2}$ of the red beads are removed from the box, what will be the new ratio of the number of red beads to the number of green beads?

29. The ratio of Suhua's money to Meilin's money was 2 : 3 at first. After Meilin spent $30, the ratio became 3 : 4. How much money did Meilin have at first?

*30. Meihua, Sufen and Liling shared a sum of money. Meihua received 20% of the money. The rest of the money was divided between Sufen and Liling in the ratio 2 : 3. If Liling received $120, how much money did Meihua receive?

31. A car took 2 hours to travel from Town A to Town B at an average speed of 60 km/h. How long would it take for the same journey if it travelled at an average speed of 80 km/h?

*32. At 12.00 noon, Henry left Town P and cycled towards Town Q at 15 km/h. At 12.10 p.m., Paul left Town Q and cycled towards Town P at 12 km/h along the same road. If they meet each other at 12.30 p.m., find the distance between the two towns.

33. If $x = 8$, find the value of $\frac{2x - 7}{3}$.

34. David paid $10m for 3 photo albums and 2 T-shirts. Each photo album cost $2m. Find, in terms of m, the cost of each T-shirt.

35. In the figure, not drawn to scale, find ∠x.

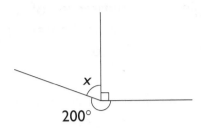

200°

36. In the figure, not drawn to scale, RP = RQ. PRS, QRT and STU are straight lines. Find ∠UTR.

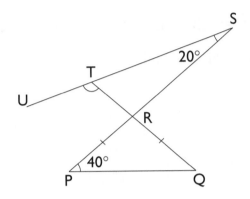

37. In the figure, not drawn to scale, CD = CE. ABCE is a parallelogram. AED is a straight line. Find ∠m.

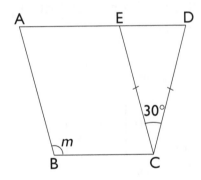

38. In the figure, P and Q are squares and R is a right-angled triangle. The areas of P and Q are 81 cm² and 25 cm² respectively. What is the area of R?

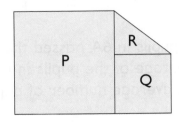

39. The figure shows a semicircular shape inside a rectangle. If the perimeter of the rectangle is 30 cm, find the perimeter of the semicircular shape. (Take $\pi = 3.14$)

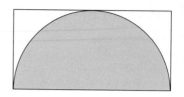

40. The base of a cuboid is a square of side 6 cm. The volume of the cuboid is 288 cm³. Find its height.

41. A rectangular tank, 20 cm long and 15 cm wide, was filled with water to a depth of 4 cm. When a stone of volume 1200 cm³ was put in the water, the water level rose to $\frac{4}{5}$ of the height of the tank. Find the height of the tank.

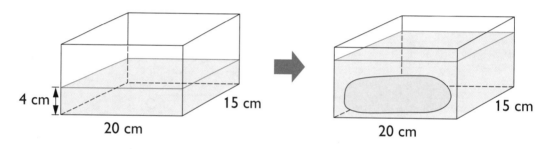

42. A school has 4 Primary Six classes. There are 40 pupils in each class. The bar graph shows the number of pupils who passed the physical fitness test in each class.

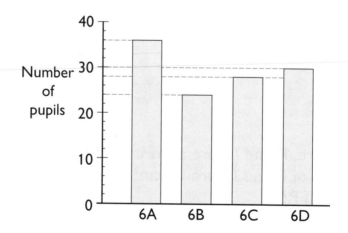

(a) How many pupils in 6A passed the physical fitness test?
(b) What percentage of the pupils in 6C failed the test?
(c) What is the average number of pupils who failed the test in each class?

REVIEW G

1. Write the following in figures.
   (a) Ten thousand and twenty-seven
   (b) Two million and twelve thousand

2. A number is smaller than 30. It is a multiple of 5. It is also a multiple of 4. What is the number?

3. The population of a town is about 108 000. Which one of the following could be the actual population?
   107 350,   107 802,   107 485,   107 097

4. Express 150 as a percentage of 500.

5. What is the weight of the papaya?

6. Express $2\frac{1}{6}$ as a decimal correct to 2 decimal places.

7. Which one of the following fractions is greater than $\frac{3}{8}$?

   $\frac{1}{3}$, $\frac{2}{5}$, $\frac{2}{7}$, $\frac{3}{10}$

8. What is the missing number in each ■?

   (a) $\frac{16}{24} = \frac{8}{■}$ (b) $\frac{6}{11} = 2 \times \frac{■}{11}$

9. A clinic opens at 8.00 a.m., but the nurses start work 15 minutes earlier. What time do the nurses start work?

10. (a) Express $1\frac{1}{4}$ hours in hours and minutes.
    (b) Express 2.3 km in kilometres and metres.

11. What is the missing number in each ■?

(a) 0.8 km = ■ m

(b) $\frac{3}{5}\ell$ = ■ ml

(c) 1.35 kg = ■ g

(d) 4.8 m = ■ m ■ cm

12. How many twenty-cent coins will make up $5?

13. 5 bottles of jam cost $12. How many bottles of jam will cost $36?

14. At a supermarket, mushrooms were sold at $0.95 per 100 g. Meihua bought 800 g of mushrooms from the supermarket. How much did she pay?

15. The average age of Mary and Peter is 30. If Mary is 6 years older than Peter, find Mary's age.

16. The table shows the postage rates for sending postcards to Malaysia and Indonesia. Find the total postage for sending 3 postcards to Malaysia and 5 postcards to Indonesia.

Country	Postage
Malaysia	30¢
Indonesia	50¢

17. Devi spent $\frac{3}{5}$ of her money on a dress. If the dress cost $48, how much money had she left?

18. Meili, Rani and Sulin shared a sum of money in the ratio 3 : 5 : 7.
    (a) What fraction of the sum of money did Rani receive? Give your answer in the simplest form.
    (b) If Rani received $150, find the sum of money shared by the three girls.

19. Find the value of 12% of $2800.

20. A storybook is sold at a discount of 20%. If the discount is $3, find the selling price of the storybook.

21. During a sale, a shop sells all its goods at a discount of 10%. Find the usual price of a basketball which is sold for $28.80.

22. Ali cycled at a speed of 12 km/h for 25 minutes. How far did he travel?

*23. Mr Li bought some oranges at 5 for $1. He also bought an equal number of apples at 4 for $1. If he paid $1 more for the apples than for the oranges, how many apples did he buy?

*24. John had twice as many stamps as Peter at first. After John bought another 15 stamps and Peter bought another 60 stamps, Peter had twice as many stamps as John. How many stamps did Peter have at first?

25. A computer club has 40 members. $\frac{1}{4}$ of them are boys. If 8 more boys join the club, what fraction of the members are boys?

26. Mary spent $\frac{2}{3}$ of her money on a skirt and a blouse. If the skirt cost twice as much as the blouse, what fraction of her money did she spend on the skirt?

27. After Gopal gave Raju $20, Gopal's money was $\frac{3}{5}$ of Raju's money. If they had $120 altogether, how much money did Gopal have at first?

*28. David and Betty each had an equal amount of money at first. After David spent $18 and Betty spent $42, Betty's money was $\frac{2}{3}$ of David's money. How much money did each of them have at first?

29. $\frac{1}{6}$ of Mr Chen's weight is equal to $\frac{2}{5}$ of Weimin's weight. Find the ratio of Mr Chen's weight to Weimin's weight.

30. The ratio of Mingli's money to Suhua's money was 3 : 2 at first. After Suhua spent $15, the ratio became 6 : 1. How much money did Suhua have at first?

*31. Peter and Mary each had an equal amount of money. After Peter spent $50 and Mary spent $\frac{1}{3}$ of her money, the ratio of Peter's money to Mary's money was 5 : 4. How much money had Peter left?

*32. John withdrew $\frac{1}{2}$ of his savings from the bank. He used 80% of the money to buy a computer. If the computer cost $2400, how much savings did he have in the bank at first?

33. Find the value of each expression when $r = 8$.

(a) $3r + \dfrac{r - 3}{5}$

(b) $2r - \dfrac{r}{2}$

34. A motorist took 2 hours to travel from Town A to Town B at an average speed of 45 km/h. If his average speed was increased by 5 km/h, how long would he take for the journey?

35. Mr Wang took 3 hours to cover the first 180 km of a journey. He took another 2 hours to cover the remaining journey at an average speed of 55 km/h. Find his average speed for the whole journey.

*36. Ahmad and Daud cycled from Town A to Town B at 12 km/h and 10 km/h respectively. Ahmad left Town A at 8.00 a.m. and arrived at Town B at 8.30 a.m. When Ahmad arrived at Town B, Daud was 1.5 km away from Town B. What time did Daud leave Town A?

37. Peter drove from Town P to Town Q. His average speed for the first $\dfrac{1}{2}$ of the journey was 60 km/h. His average speed for the remaining journey was 50 km/h. If he left Town P at 6.00 a.m., what time did he arrive at Town Q?

240 km

P   Q

38. John and Peter started jogging from the same place at the same time, but in opposite directions along a straight road. After jogging for 3 hours, they were 27 km apart. If John's average speed was 6 km/h, find Peter's average speed.

39. The figure is made up of 2 semicircular shapes, each of diameter 10 cm. Find the perimeter of the figure. (Take $\pi = 3.14$)

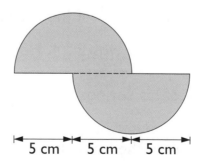

5 cm   5 cm   5 cm

40. The figure shows 4 quarter circles inside a square of side 14 cm. Find the area of the shaded part. $\left(\text{Take } \pi = \dfrac{22}{7} \right)$

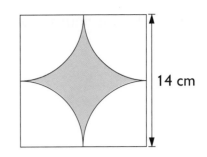

14 cm

41. The figure is made up of two squares. Find the shaded area in the figure.

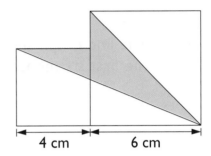

4 cm   6 cm

42. The figure is made up of a right-angled triangle and a semicircle. Find its area. $\left(\text{Take } \pi = \dfrac{22}{7} \right)$

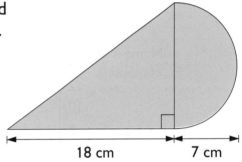

18 cm   7 cm

43. The base of an empty rectangular tank measures 50 cm by 40 cm. A stone of volume 3000 cm³ is placed in the tank. When 33 litres of water are poured into the tank, the tank is $\dfrac{2}{3}$ full. Find the height of the tank. (1 litre = 1000 cm³)

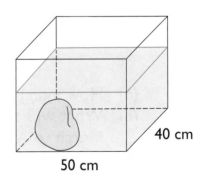

40 cm

50 cm

44. In the figure, not drawn to scale, QT = RT. PQR and PUS are straight lines. Find ∠RPS.

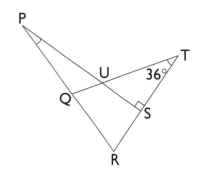

99

45. In the figure, not drawn to scale, AD // BC and CE = CD. Find ∠x.

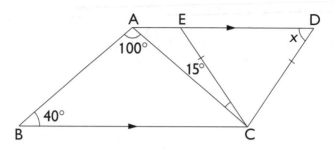

46. The line graph shows the number of computers sold in a shop during the first six months of a year.

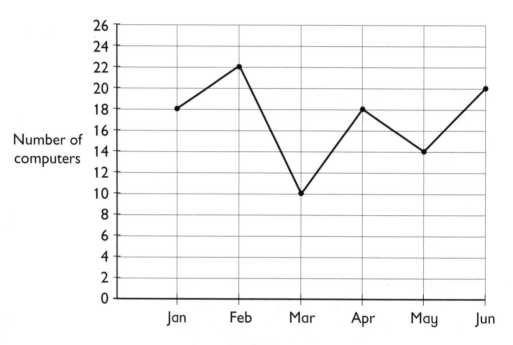

(a) How many computers were sold in February?
(b) What was the increase in the number of computers sold from March to April?
(c) What was the average number of computers sold per month?

ANSWERS

Practice 1A
1. 62.8 cm
2. 220 cm
3. 72.2 cm
4. 25.12 cm
5. 88 cm
6. 20π cm

Practice 1B
1. 113.04 cm²
2. 616 m²
3. (a) 12.56 cm   (b) 12.56 cm²
4. 1.57 m²
5. 78.5 cm²
6. Area = 28.26 cm²
   Circumference = 18.84 cm
7. 154 cm²

Practice 1C
1. (a) 504 cm²   (b) 88 cm
2. Area = 63.25 m²
   Perimeter = 29.7 m
3. Area = 38.88 cm²
   Perimeter = 36.56 cm
4. Area = 2π m²
   Perimeter = 3π m
5. 12π cm²

Review A
1. Two million, three hundred and forty thousand
2. 0.57
3. 2
4. 7
5. 0.09, 0.123, 0.25, 0.5
6. 5.59 kg
7. $\dfrac{1}{8}$
8. $\dfrac{3}{8}$
9. 2
10. 21.49
11. 600.93
12. 41.86
13. 17
14. 35 000
15. 67.5
16. (a) 80 min   (b) 20 g
17. 8
18. $200
19. 26
20. 0.32 kg
21. 38 kg

22. 36 kg
23. $\dfrac{7}{20}$
24. $\dfrac{4}{9}$
25. $20
26. 360
27. 4
28. 25%
29. 25%
30. $28
31. 120 km
32. $240
33. $7.15
34. $860
35. $960
36. 3 : 4
37. $2000
38. $120
39. 12.5 km/h
40. (a) $2\dfrac{1}{3}$ (b) 36
41. $\dfrac{3x-2}{2}$ kg
42. 81 cm²
43. 45.7 cm
44. D
45.
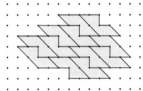
46. (a) Thursday   (b) 5%   (c) 37
47. (a) 18%   (b) $\dfrac{1}{5}$ (c) 150

Review B
1. 4
2. 1000
3. (a) 10 000   (b) 0.06
4. 36
5. 2.53
6. 9.009
7. $\dfrac{1}{3}$
8. 1000
9. (a) $\dfrac{6}{125}$ (b) $\dfrac{9}{25}$

10. $\frac{12}{25}$, $\frac{3}{5}$, $\frac{62}{100}$, $\frac{31}{20}$

11. (a) 4   (b) 40
12. 100
13. 11 h 15 min
14. 16
15. 850 g
16. 60
17. 8
18. 16
19. 41
20. 25 min

21. $\frac{1}{6}$

22. $\frac{5}{8}$

23. (a) 12   (b) 7
24. 35 m
25. 12%
26. 75%
27. $4.50
28. 1.25 m/s
29. 10
30. $10
31. 16
32. 24
33. 50 kg
34. $240
35. 18%
36. 25%
37. 85 km/h
38. 48 cm²
39. 57.5 cm²
40. 31.4 cm
41.

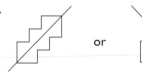

or

42. 9
43. C
44. (a) 40   (b) 25%   (c) 8
    (d) 80
45. (a) $1800   (b) $1880   (c) 600

Practice 3A
1. 36 cm²
2. 8 cm
3. (a) 4   (b) 8
4. (a) 27 cm³   (b) 324 cm³
5. (a) 32 cm³   (b) 72 cm²

Practice 3B
1. 4.5 cm
2. 10.8 m
3. (a) 168 ℓ   (b) 21 min
4. 40 cm

Practice 3C
1. 11.6 cm
2. (a) 105 000 cm³   (b) 8750 cm³
3. 6.5 min
4. 6000 cm³

Practice 4A
1. ∠a = 50°   ∠b = 58°
2. ∠p = 38°   ∠q = 104°
3. 80°
4. 82°
5. 66°

Practice 4B
1. ∠p = 60°   ∠q = 124°
2. ∠a = 34°   ∠b = 56°
3. ∠x = 125°   ∠y = 27.5°
4. 24°
5. 40°

Review C
1. (a) 30 030   (b) 3 040 000
2. (a) 100   (b) 0.09
3. 3400   4. 6
5. $33\frac{1}{3}$ 6. $690
7. $\frac{2}{9}$ 8. 54 ℓ
9. 8 : 2 : 5   10. 6 : 1
11. $\frac{5}{3}$ 12. 40%
13. 15%   14. 40%
15. $\frac{1}{40}$ 16. $2.90
17. 4 km/h   18. $75
19. 135 ℓ
20. (a) 1 : 2   (b) 20
21. 96 cm²   22. 54 km/h
23. 80 km/h   24. 4t − 2
25. $(40 − 3n)   26. 60°
27. 22.5°   28. 80°
29. 60.5 cm²   30. 6π m²
31. 8 cm   32. 1.8 min
33. (a) 2.2 ℓ   (b) C   (c) $\frac{3}{5}$

Review D

1. (a) 600   (b) 1000
2. (a) 8   (b) 50
3. 13.28
4. (a) 0.375   (b) 0.82
5. $\frac{3}{15}$
6. 1.4
7. 9.25 a.m.
8. (a) $\frac{2}{25}$ (b) $4\frac{7}{25}$
9. (a) 32%   (b) 45%
10. $\frac{11}{80}$
11. 36%
12. (a) 5   (b) 6 : 9 : 15
13. $5   14. $244
15. $\frac{11}{18}$ 16. $\frac{1}{3}$
17. $4.50   18. $340
19. (a) $38.50   (b) $60
20. 5 min   21. 181
22. 140   23. $150
24. 7 : 4 : 3   25. 140
26. 2 : 1 : 3   27. $120
28. 21%   29. 10.24 a.m.
30. 4 km/h   31. $11a + 3$
32. 307 cm²   33. 3 cm
34. 106°   35. C
36.
37. (a) 50 ℓ (b) 150 ℓ (c) $230

Review E

1. 0.8   2. 26 000
3. 40   4. 430 g
5. $\frac{3}{5}$ 6. $\frac{4}{5}$
7. 0.08   8. $2\frac{2}{25}$
9. 2 m, $2\frac{1}{4}$ m,   2.49 m,   2.6 m
10. $\frac{3}{8}$ 11. 8
12. $30   13. $6.50
14. 2025   15. 9
16. 12   17. 6
18. 3 : 2   19. 48 kg
20. $48   21. 6.25%

22. 12   23. 1500
24. 60 km   25. 40
26. 90¢   27. $3.50
28. $270   29. $225
30. 1.2 kg   31. 5 : 8
32. 50   33. $5x + 36$
34. 24 cm   35. 75 cm²
36. 41.4 cm   37. 192 cm³
38. 40 cm   39. 37°
40. 85°   41. 9
42. (a) $\frac{1}{4}$ (b) $\frac{1}{8}$ (c) 960

Practice 5A

1. 132   2. $20
3. $22   4. $7.15
5. $21   6. 12
7. $15   8. 195
9. $480   10. 28

Practice 5B

1. $36   2. $20
3. 20   4. $480
5. 12   6. $300
7. $30   8. 5

Practice 5C

1. 225   2. $56
3. $225   4. 90
5. 0.9 kg   6. $168
7. $12   8. $100

Practice 5D

1. 5 : 6   2. 48
3. 60   4. 1176 g
5. 15 cm   6. $37.50
7. 2 : 1   8. 5 : 12
9. 9 : 5   10. 4 : 5

Practice 5E

1. 6 : 1   2. 8 : 5
3. $48   4. 120
5. $140   6. 600 ml
7. 28   8. $140
9. $32

Practice 5F

1. 500   2. 68%
3. 82   4. 50%
5. 60%   6. 80%
7. $800   8. 76
9. $150   10. $26

Practice 5G
1. 4.45 p.m.
2. 95 km/h
3. 48 km/h
4. 50 km/h
5. $1\frac{1}{4}$ h
6. 8.50 a.m.
7. 2 km

Review F
1. (a) 356 000   (b) 4.3
2. 0.103
3. $\frac{3}{8}$
4. $\frac{9}{200}$
5. 24
6. $4\frac{1}{6}$
7. (a) 16   (b) $\frac{19}{20}$
8. (a) 1000   (b) 1000
9. 75¢
10. $96\frac{1}{2}$% or 96.5%
11. (a) 4 : 5   (b) 80%
12. (a) $\frac{3}{8}$ (b) $\frac{5}{3}$
13. $52.50
14. $800
15. 6 h
16. $16
17. 61
18. $\frac{5}{12}$
19. 42.5 kg
20. $\frac{7}{16}$
21. 60%
22. 40%
23. 20
24. 54 km
25. 4
26. $25
27. $120
28. 3 : 4

29. $270
30. $50
31. 1.5 h or $1\frac{1}{2}$ h
32. 11.5 km
33. 3
34. $2m$
35. 70°
36. 120°
37. 105°
38. 10 cm²
39. 25.7 cm
40. 8 cm
41. 10 cm
42. (a) 36   (b) 30%   (c) 10.5

Review G
1. (a) 10 027   (b) 2 012 000
2. 20
3. 107 802
4. 30%
5. 450 g
6. 2.17
7. $\frac{2}{5}$
8. (a) 12   (b) 3
9. 7.45 a.m.
10. (a) 1 h 15 min   (b) 2 km 300 m
11. (a) 800 m   (b) 600 ml
    (c) 1350 g   (d) 4 m 80 cm
12. 25
13. 15
14. $7.60
15. 33
16. $3.40
17. $32
18. (a) $\frac{1}{3}$ (b) $450
19. $336
20. $12
21. $32
22. 5 km
23. 20
24. 10
25. $\frac{3}{8}$
26. $\frac{4}{9}$
27. $65
28. $90
29. 12 : 5
30. $20
31. $250
32. $6000
33. (a) 25   (b) 12
34. $1\frac{4}{5}$ h
35. 58 km/h
36. 8.03 a.m.
37. 10.24 a.m.
38. 3 km/h
39. 41.4 cm
40. 42 cm²
41. 14 cm²
42. 203 cm²
43. 27 cm
44. 18°
45. 55°
46. (a) 22   (b) 8   (c) 17